Pictorial history of
Japanese Motorcycles

Published 1997 by Uitgeverij Elmar B.V.
Delftweg 147, 2289 BD Rijswijk, Holland
in association with Bay View Books Ltd.
The Red House, 25-26 Bridgeland Street,
Bideford Devon EX39 2PZ

ISBN 1 870979 97 4

Design and typesetting A/Z grafisch serviceburo b.v.
Den Haag, the Netherlands
Printed in Italy

PICTORIAL
HISTORY OF
JAPANESE
MOTORCYCLES

Cornelis Vandenheuvel

CONTENTS

PREFACE

Mr Honda: made transportation history comparable to Henry Ford's achievements.

Approximately 80 per cent of the motorcycles in existence today have been put together in a Japanese factory. Managing directors of renowned European – especially British – firms refused to acknowledge the immense qualities of Japanese bikes; and when they did, it was too late to match them. Consequently, motorcycle history is being shaped by the Japanese today. Motorcycling has been led by the French, the British and the German, in that order, since the turn of the twentieth century. No-one will deny that beautiful European and American classic motorcycles exist. But there are, also, beautiful Japanese classics. It is possible to appreciate a Harley Duo Glide next to a Norton 99 and a Honda CB 450; and there is nothing inferior about an NSU Max. Some people seem to think that if you like one machine you have to dislike the other. This book covers the Japanese motorcycle from just after World War Two. The important models in each period are described. A special thank you goes to photographer Wout Meppelink. Humour and quality of work can go hand in hand, as shown by this man. You, the reader, won't be able to hear him tell a joke – but his pictures in this book speak for themselves.

THE MOST DEPENDABLE MOTOR CYCLE,
DREAM 250, 350, HONDA 200, BENLY 125

HONDA MOTOR CO., LTD.

NO. 5, 5-CHOME, YAESU, CHUO-KU, TOKYO, JAPAN.
TEL: (28) 7331   CABLE ADDRESS   "HONDAMOTOR"

August, 1957

OUTLINE OF COMPANY

NAME OF COMPANY:	Honda Motor Co.,Ltd.
Address:	5, 5-chome, Yaesu, Chuo-ku, Tokyo.
Branch Offices:	Tokyo, Osaka, Nagoya, Fukuoka, Sapporo.
Established in:	September, 1948.
Capital:(Paid-up)	¥360,000,000.00 (Equivalent to US$1,000,000.-)
Representatives:	President: Soichiro Honda Manag. Director: Takeo Fujisawa Sales Manager: Kensuke Takahashi
Bank Reference:	The Mitsubishi Bank Ltd. The Sanwa Bank Ltd.
No. of Employees:	2,418 (Male: 1,714 Female: 704)

Plant:

	Site	Bldg. Site	Machineries	Equip.
Saitama Plant	109,254 sq.m	21,450 sq.m	563	213
Hamamatsu Plant	59,720	9,100	390	102
	168,974 sq.m	30,550 sq.m	953	315

Note:

Machineries include 102 sets of foreign-made
high precision machines amounting to more than
One Million dollars which were imported from
U.S.A. West Germany and Switzerlandfor the
past five years.
Equipments means such devices and instalations
as chrome-plating, painting, heat treatment,
assembly line (conveyers), testing, power
station, etc.

Goods Manufactured:	(A) Motorcycles DREAM 350 & 250 c.c. BENLY 125 c.c. (B) Gasoline Engine VN & VNA 3.5HP

Average Output:
(June & July 1957)

(A) DREAM   3,513 units per month
     BENLY   3,835 units per month
(B) VN & VNA 1,000 units per month

This letter – of which the page shown here is a part – triggered Dutch motorcycle importers to go to Japan and come back with an agreement. At the time the agreement was considered valid for all of Europe; the Japanese thought that Europe had the same political structure as the US.

THE FIFTIES
SCHOOLTIME

When the dust clouds of World War Two had cleared, Japan had to start from scratch. The entire infrastructure, never well developed in pre-war days, had been destroyed. Apart from Japan's ruthless ability to fight modern warfare, we knew little about this far-off country. General opinion was that the Japanese made toys and radios of poor quality. The only saving grace for these products was their low cost. Post war ,only Japanese cameras established a reputation for good quality.

In the USA, some servicemen returning home brought with them motorcycles they had purchased in Japan. There didn't seem to be any reason to pay great attention to these rarities, in the early fifties. The machines were clones of European designs – sometimes of pre-war designs. Most of them were small fry, not more than 250cc. The big exception was Rikuo, who were building copies of pre-war Harleys. But with the exception of the Japanese police, nobody was in the market for Rikuo motorcycles. The real thing, the Harley-Davidson, was widely available in the USA – a land where they're inclined to say: "There is no substitute for cubic inches". If an American wanted a more sporty bike than a Harley, he would buy a Triumph or a Norton or a BSA. The whole phenomenon of motorcycling was considered to be something for people on the fringe of society, anyway. America certainly was not waiting for the Japanese and their little runabouts.

In Europe, things were different. There was a broader acceptance of motorcycles, and there were more motorcyclists. Where a young American would buy a gas-guzzling automobile, his European counterpart would buy an old moped, and, when he was a little older, a motorcycle.

Motorcycle riders were divided roughly into two categories. There were the fans of the traditional British makes. Although they were very divided as to which particular firm they supported, they at least agreed on one thing: a motorcycle had to be British. Norton men wouldn't be seen dead on, for example, a BSA; let alone ride it. If you didn't fancy a 'made in

England' bike, there were the Continental makes. Germany was a big name in motorcycling in those days. The Italians, however, did not do much exporting. They had their hands full in the home market. It was in the sixties that Italy entered the world market.

Belgian manufacturers generally followed the British line. FN and Sarolea were the exceptions. Much the same can be said about the French and Swiss makes. The French, who had a very rich motorcycle history, never recovered from the war in a 'motorcycling' sense. So, if you quantify the European market in the early fifties, there were either German bikes of high quality and advanced design or British machines with a long tradition and a high performance. British bikes had plenty of cubic capacity, charisma and performance, but were behind in technology. The technical heyday of the British lay further back, in the 1920s and 1930s. During that period almost any design we now know was at least tried out in Britain. German bikes had quality and were of modern construction, but they didn't have looks and appeal. And capacity and performance generally did not match the Brit bikes.

HONDA
A型

Honda's A model, built after Tohatsu generator engines were no longer available. Belt drive was smooth, but of course outdated.

We may conclude, therefore, that there was at least some public interest in motorcycles in Europe. In 1951 the first pleas for more development began to appear in the specialist magazines. There were novelties like the telescopic-fork Triumph Speed Twin, the BSA A7 and the Norton 500 twin, but the majority of the bikes offered were developments of pre-war designs; and this was beginning to show. In 1957 this situation still had not really changed. The motorcycle magazines searched very hard for new developments to describe. It was then that Italy came into the picture with Mondial, Benelli, Parilla and many more. Then, in 1957, the Dutch weekly magazine *Motor* became interested in Japan. They were wondering if there were motorcycle factories over there worth investigating. The editors had come across a 300-page Japanese magazine. They could not read it, but the pictures seemed interesting! The Dutch speculated on the poor quality of the Japanese products they knew. *Motor* didn't realise it, but they had a scoop that would not be matched in a very long time. They got answers from factories by the name of Lilac and Emuro – and a letter from a Mister Honda. Part of this letter can still be found in Motor's archives. It is dated August 1957.

The news spread round the world. It was a *Motor* article, based on information forthcoming in 1957, that stimulated ambitious businessmen to go to Japan. The Dutch and the British were introduced to Mr Honda's products two years later. Independently, the US started importing Hondas in 1959. In this case the initiative came from the Honda Motor Company itself which opened an American office in 1959. Mr. Honda's contacts with Europe in fact dated from as early as 1954, albeit unnoticed by the press. The bikes described in the 1956 and 1957 brochures sent to *Motor* turned out to be very modern indeed. When the specifications of Meguro, Lilac, Pointer and Honda motorcycles became known, European cynicism dwindled.

Nowadays we find it quite normal to speak of the Big Four – Honda, Kawasaki, Suzuki and Yamaha. It could almost have been the Big Five. Before we come to that, however, let's go back to early post-war days in Japan, to the story of the Japanese version of the Wirtschaftwunder (economic miracle) that happened in Germany after the war.

The Japanese had been forced to enter the twentieth century directly after the war. Previously they had lived in a totally different world, which in some cases could be compared to the European Middle Ages. They turned out to be able to adapt very quickly, and effectively. They took over the methods and organising ways of the occupying Americans. But they didn't just copy. They added Japanese logic. Nobody ever had to teach a Japanese to work hard! It is incredible how dedicated to his work a Japanese is. In Western eyes it would not be fitting to have an employer interfere with the private life of a worker; in Japan such interference was not only accepted, it was quite normal. In Japan you would be loyal to your employer almost till death did you part. The very existence of a worker is at the service of the company he works for. In Japan unions play a very different role from their equivalent in Europe or the USA. If there is a strike, it is generally during work hours: the people have a ribbon around their arm saying: "We are on strike". But meanwhile, work goes on! The directors of a company would, in their turn, react as if there was a real strike in progress. Everything happened as in the West, but with the addition of Japanese logic. The labour conflict was fought out as in America, but without loss of production. On the other hand, the managerial staff of a company were far more interested in the well-being of the people who worked in the company. There was a sort of 'honour' among the Japanese that Westerners will probably never understand to the full. Very soon Japan's economy was growing at an

Adler's MB 250 S showed the way to go for to many Japanese makers, including Suzuki and Yamaha. It was probably the best two-stroke around in 1954.

(left) Lilac was ahead of the field in 1951 with this 150cc shaft drive model LB. Masashi Ito was proud of his "chainless motorcycles".

(right) This A model engine was built by Soichiro Honda in a shed; 20 years later things had changed for Mr Honda...

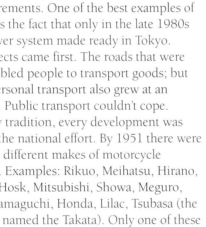

astonishing pace. Always public needs went before personal requirements. One of the best examples of this approach is the fact that only in the late 1980s was a good sewer system made ready in Tokyo. Industrial projects came first. The roads that were being built enabled people to transport goods; but the need for personal transport also grew at an incredible rate. Public transport couldn't cope. Unhindered by tradition, every development was absorbed into the national effort. By 1951 there were more than 100 different makes of motorcycle manufacturers. Examples: Rikuo, Meihatsu, Hirano, Tohatsu, Fuji, Hosk, Mitsubishi, Showa, Meguro, Pointer, SJK, Yamaguchi, Honda, Lilac, Tsubasa (the top model was named the Takata). Only one of these would be familiar to today's motorcyclist. We will now describe some of the manufacturers that were in business in the early fifties.

This Myata 250 is a mixture of Adler and Puch. The frame is Puch-like and the engine has much in common with an Adler. It died in the 1960s when the firm failed to follow Yamaha and Suzuki's development lead.

Rikuo

The factory that was allowed to sell to the American administration was considered the most prestigious, and after the war, this honour went to Rikuo. The firm built a large variety of machines but big side-valve V-twins assembled as a consequence of a licence agreement with Harley-Davidson were the mainstream models. But very soon Rikuo were making improvements; in 1948 the telescopic front fork appeared (Harley still had a few years to go without teles). Automatic spark advance was next. Then came a positive-change four-speed gearbox; foot-operated, too (Harley still used a hand-change). Finally, Rikuo felt they were no longer obliged to pay for the licence agreement, but this rebellion was not tolerated. The Americans did not have to pressure the Japanese authorities to take steps; they understood themselves, and 'leaned' on Rikuo. The police contract was withdrawn, and very soon, the firm was dwindling into obscurity. Although the company appeared in sales lists until approximately 1962, development of the side-valve came to a halt in 1953. Rikuo did not survive the great battle that was to come. At the end of this, in 1959, there were only about 18 makes left, of which no more than six had a chance of surviving.

Meguro

This too was a company that followed traditional ways. Again, in the Japanese fashion. It was 1953 when Meguro purchased a 500cc BSA A 7. The Meguro K 500 Stamina looked very much like a BSA: it worked like a BSA, handled and felt like a BSA. That's the copying part of the story. When it came to technology, there was something different going on. The BSA's built-up crankshaft relied on small ball bearings and a bronze bush. The big-end bearings were split, with car-type liners. Oil entered the

crankshaft, and the main bearing, then fed the big-ends. The heavy central flywheel caused the crank to flex at higher revolutions. When the BSA was still a 500 there was no problem, but that would change when it grew to 650 cc. The Meguro arranged things very differently. Two large ball bearings supported the Meguro's crank with its broad-base tappets. The needle rollers of the one-piece conrods received plenty of oil. The mains were fed from channels from the tappets. The Meguro central flywheel was far smaller and lighter than the BSA's, with heavy outer webs on the crank, next to the main bearings. Far less flexing of a better-lubricated crankshaft was the result – the Meguro having a shorter stroke than the BSA. A BSA performed better on the road than a Meguro; but the latter was far ahead as far as quality was concerned.

The Meguro was one of the best Japanese motorcycles of the early fifties, and very popular among police officers. Meguro also built 175 and 250 cc singles. They were not great performers but, like the 500, their quality was very impressive. A range of 50 cc two-strokes came out bearing the Meguro logo and these too were of excellent quality; however, in spite of their modern design they didn't really make it.

Putting aside the highly successful Meguro 500, however, it is fair to say that the Japanese motorcycles were still mainly of inferior quality when compared with European machinery. Halfway through the 1950s, the Japanese motorcycle industry could be likened to an ants' nest! Hundreds of mostly small companies were competing, merging, copying and doing whatever they had to do to survive. Many of these makers simply bought a European machine and copied it. Sometimes they copied each other. A motorcycle could be a copy of a copy of a copy! Most of the European examples bought by Japanese factories came from Germany, not from Britain. Even French and Italian design influence can be traced in a Japanese creation. While writing this book I came across a copy of the catalogue that *Motor* of Holland received in the 50s. What a treasure! More than 100 makes were listed. Many were copies – clones – of German models, especially the DKW RT 125. I reiterate that in the early fifties all the age-old prejudices against Japanese motorcycles were largely true. They were 'non-performing' copies that easily fell apart. But this wasn't to be the case for long. Around 1955, Japanese people stopped buying 'anything'. They still were not allowed to buy foreign bikes. Only

factories were given a licence to import foreign machines, for purposes of study.

The seller's market had become a buyer's market. In 1959, the first year in which the makers exported from Japan, it could be said that Japanese bikes were no longer clones. In fact, by then only two bikes were seen as having European parentage: the Lilac and the Kawasaki W 1. A Yamaha XS 650 displays almost all the characteristics of a Triumph Bonneville, yet there is no real evidence of copying. Ironically, around this period it was possible to adduce signs of some Europeans copying the Japanese! The Laverda 750 and the Benelli 750 Sei owe their existance to Honda's CB 72 and 500 Four. Not to mention the John Bloor Triumphs, which can be traced back to the Kawasaki GPZ 900 R. There was nothing wrong with all this, of course. Not many people actually saw with their own eyes a motorcycle from Japan they could call non-original, ie, a copy. This may be a little hard to accept for die-hard fans of European classic motorcycles; yet I suggest it is true.

Honda
Mr. Soichiro Honda was a man who had a very special way of dealing with problems. After a

During the 1950s Meguro was an important manufacturer and offered a range of neat models. Their K 500 Stamina went into the sixties as the 650 Kawasaki.

relatively successful period of automobile racing in the 1930s ended in a big crash in a Ford, he started his own workshop. These days we would call it a service centre. He called it a Technical Research Centre, and in fact that is what it was. Soichiro used it to teach himself everything he wanted to learn. Within a few years he understood far more about engineering techniques than the average Japanese manufacturer. When he found that car manufacturers were badly in need of piston rings, he tried to establish his own piston ring factory. But there was one big problem for Mr. Honda: he knew nothing about piston rings other than that they were the round things you find in close company with pistons. Honda's first piston rings were useless. This was the first time Honda had not managed to acquire the knowledge he needed. So he went back to school again. A few months before examinations were due, Honda left the school. People asked him whether he'd left because he feared the exams. The answer was typical of Soichiro Honda: "I have learned what I wanted to know. I don't need a certificate to prove that. There's no need to waste any more time with exams". Back to business. Quite a no-nonsense approach, wouldn't you say?

The war came and went, and Honda had to start all over again, like the rest of Japan. In 1946 Soichiro bought a stock of surplus generator engines (made by: Tohatsu) from the army. He managed to adapt the engines to run on what was charitably classified as gasoline. In 1947 bicycles with these engines were the first Honda motorcycles to be sold to the public. When the supply of the army engines dried up, Honda built his first engine, a 50cc two-stroke that

Soichiro Honda had a dream. This emblem is from a (never exported) 1955 SA 250; or possibly an SB 350 single.

could be clipped to a bicycle. The Honda Cub was born. The thing would often only start after much pedalling. Once running, it produced a smoke screen that today would have the rider branded a hooligan; but in 1951 nobody was bothered. Since these Honda engines, soon nicknamed 'the chimney' engines, did not blow up immediately, they were considered to be of good quality.

But even then, when people were prepared to buy just about anything on wheels, Soichiro Honda felt the need to improve. Many of his competitors didn't. Honda knew his own shortcomings as far as marketing was concerned. His partner Kawashima, however, had an accurate perception of the consumer's requirements. Both men had great respect for each other's complementary qualities. The result was that Kawashima drew up the list of requirements for the new model, and Honda translated these into technical modifications.

The next model was the D Dream, a 125cc four-stroke. The engine had a strong NSU flavour to it, while the frame was clearly inspired by the Zündapp motorcycles of the 1940s. Performance was very modest – certainly not as good as that of contemporary European designs. However, in post-war Japan there was no use for high-performance machines. What mattered was getting from one town to another, while carrying 100 kilograms of luggage, over the unpaved tracks that passed for roads. You had to manage it on as little fuel as possible, because you never knew whether you would find a gas station. Things went well for Honda. Still, at that stage he was one of the smaller companies ….

Lilac

One of the more important Japanese marques in the early fifties was Lilac, part of the Marusho company led by Masashi Ito. The name was chosen for quite banal reasons; Ito's wife was very fond of lilac

The 50cc Meguros were very "modern" in 1958. In that year, however, the Honda C 100 Super Cub became available.

flowers, and the name 'sounded fashionable'. Western names were in vogue in those days. The company was founded in 1951. The word Marusho may be roughly translated as 'the search for the perfect motorcycle'. Ito had co-opted this vision from his former master, who was … Soichiro Honda!

Ito started out well, with modified copies of Honda D and E Dreams, together with a very BMW-like 250 single with shaft-drive. Shaft-drive was to become a typical Lilac feature. (Ito was very proud of his 'chainless motorcycles'.) A 90cc two-stroke, the Baby-Lilac, was not successful; but that was an exception. The 1954 350cc TW side-valve flat twin, the Dragon, was a very rugged bike which acquired a great name for reliability.

All these bikes were built in many varieties. They weren't high performers by European standards, but their modest power and speed were acceptable in Japan. It was a Lilac SY 250 single that won the very first Asama race held in 1955.

Lilac stood for quality, by Japanese standards, but it has to be said that Ito was in fact merely lucky. Although the (translated) name of the company might suggest 'perfection', Ito didn't quite live up to the goal described. He would buy a foreign, or other Japanese, bike, copy it, incorporate some improvements, and dump it on the market. He had the luck to pick a few good examples, and he had no major disasters with new bikes. But his drive for improvement was not as strong as that of his former teacher, Mr. Honda.

With a seller's market, and with this good fortune of his in copying the right bikes, Ito seemed to have it made by 1955. But things were to change. Success drove Ito to design yet another series of motorcycles (still not of original design) that would be really modern, and good enough for export. These new Victoria-like V-twins were to be built in a completely new factory. Models would range from 125cc to 350cc. The older Lilac models were abandoned and the old factory was sold. All finances were allocated to the construction of the brand-new factory, to be built in 1959. And then, disaster! The builder went bankrupt during construction of the new factory. Ito's money vanished like snow melting in the sun, and suddenly the company was in desperate trouble. His old master, Honda, helped out by giving him orders as a sub-contractor for some parts, so he didn't have to start begging. (Ito had previously refused a merger with Colleda – later to become Suzuki – simply out of loyalty to Honda,

and now Honda had paid back this loyalty.) The bank helped out, too, after Honda convinced them that Ito was a safe investment. All this occurred to a backdrop of severe fall-out in the Japanese motorcycle industry.

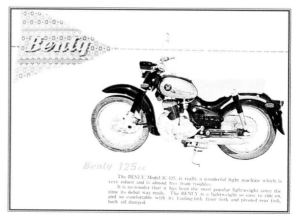

Honda development in the early fifties is shown in these three illustrations. The NSU Fox was copied in 1952, to begin with, but then Honda started improving. The Benly JA of 1953 had a pivot behind the engine (moving with the rear fork) and slim teles up front. The 1954 JB used an Earles front fork and 'normal' rear suspension. The 1956 JC had the then fashionable leading-link fork.

Development of the larger Hondas proceeded alongside the Benly models. The SB 350 of 1954 with teles was followed by the 1955 MF 350. Nobody could ever explain the big exhaust downpipe, more usually a feature of two-strokes like the German TWN.

In 1960, the bank allowed Ito a second loan on top of the first one. A year later, the new factory, with the double financial burden, was ready and Ito started producing 250cc LS 18 V-twins as fast as the assembly line could run. Not testing, as before; just producing, in order to generate revenue to pay off the debts. It all went badly wrong, as we shall see in the chapter on the 1960s.

Tohatsu

Tohatsu was the biggest motorcycle company in Japan during the 50s. They had examined the DKW factory in Germany, and built various small 'strokers' from 50 to 250 cc. All were well built, but none was exceptional. In Europe during the early fifties, DKW was a leading factory, although the company's real achievements dated back to pre-war days. After the war, DKW was unable to match its pre-war successes and status. (Tohatsu was in fact to go the same way during the 50s.) The motorcycle department at Tohatsu was only a small part of a big parent company, and the directors did not have the inspirational calibre of a Soichiro Honda, Masashi Ito or Shunzo Suzuki. Where some companies took big

steps forward towards the end of the decade, Tohatsu just went on with what they had done. Later 50 and 125cc twin two-stroke engines would appear, powering many a racing bike. Kazuo 'Johnny' Honda (no relative) was one of the better known Tohatsu factory riders. As for the company as a whole, there was no real 'drive'. More was required than mere assembling. Johnny Honda tried hard, but he was certainly not of the calibre of his namesake. The racing department went on developing the twin-cylinder racers even as the company was fading into oblivion. Tohatsu went bankrupt in early 1964. Almost the entire Tohatsu race department went to Bridgestone, taking designs and a complete machine as a sort of package deal to the new employer. Some went along with Johnny Honda to produce their own racing machines under the name of JRM, with a number of the 50 and 125cc twin engines being sold in Holland. At the time, Kazuo was marketing modified Kyokuto four-stroke single-cylinder speedway engines in Holland under the name of Eicoh. The Kyokuto was a single-overhead-camshaft unit, converted by Kazuo Honda to double-overhead cams, and bearing some resemblance to both ESO and BSA designs. Looking old-fashioned as speedway engines normally do, the Japanese engines were powerful, albeit at higher revs than traditional speedway engines. Only very recently one of these engines has surfaced in Holland. Until then not a single unit was believed to have survived.

Meihatsu

One of the few Japanese disciples of the British line of motorcycles was Meihatsu whose story shows similarities with that of Tohatsu. It was part of the huge Kawasaki Heavy Industries Group, building 350 and 500 four-stroke singles that could easily pass as an earlier British AJS. Well built; but nothing special, without any advanced technical features. In short, they were merely mediocre copies of outdated AJS and Matchless bikes, acceptable in 1955, but not in 1960. Like Tohatsu, Meihatsu did not have an inspirational leader, and would have probably gone bankrupt if a rich benefactor had not decided to step in. The leaders of Kawasaki's Aircraft Division decided they wanted a motorcycle department: Meihatsu and Meguro were to join forces under the Kawasaki banner.

Yamaha

Taraguchi Yamaha was a manufacturer of musical organs who made a journey of 125 miles by foot

Lilac made many models in the fifties. This SV 350 Dragon had outstanding qualities but was not a good looker.

Lilac KD 150 of 1952. At this stage Lilac was perhaps ahead of Honda.

Lilac SY 250 single. One of these machines won its class in the first Asama race, in 1955.

carrying an organ in order to get official approval to start making them on a regular basis. This was back in the 'medieval' Japan of the 19th century. His initial application was unsuccessful, but on the second attempt (and journey) he got the stamp of approval that he sought. Taraguchi founded the Nippon Gakki (Japanese Instruments) firm and the business prospered. Soon Nippon Gakki was the biggest instrument maker in Japan. During the second world war they made parts for aircraft, including wooden propellers, as well as various parts for other factories. Motorcycles were never even considered until around 1953, when the directors decided they couldn't ignore the market for personal transport. Having seen the hectic developments in the industry since 1951, the company came up with a plan, a vision: the Nippon Gakki motorcycles were to bear the name of the founder of the company, Yamaha. The company's emblem made sure that the connection with the musical factory was carried through, to honour the efforts of Taragushi Yamaha in establishing the firm. They started in a vary cautious way, copying a

motorcycle that had proven pedigree. The leaders knew that this copying could not last, but they preferred to start this way rather than risk an entirely original design. They had seen enough of that already. The first bike chosen to copy was DKW's RT 125.

The 1955 Yamaha YA 1, nicknamed the Red Dragon, was not very special, because it hardly differed from the original. But quality was good, as with the DKW. Some members of the staff, with no technical knowledge, made a 125-mile trip on the prototypes. The trip went smoothly for the bike; the appalling weather and the bad roads made it hell for the riders. The bikes' excellent performance resulted in an immediate opening of production. Soon a 175 cc version (again like DKW) followed.

Glory for Lilac: the UY 2 single. Well built and reliable, these models sold well. They were fast, too.

Tohatsu, as built at the end of the fifties. The marque was already lagging behind the opposition. This rare sales brochure dates from 1959. As far as can be traced, no Tohatsus were sold outside Japan.

(left) Pointer: another ultimate failure. This is the 1962 sales brochure, issued in the USA. Some Pointers were sold, but very few. The end for Pointer came in 1964.

(right) Bridgestone survived with the models on offer in the late fifties, but only thanks to the umbrella provided by the tyre department. After 1964 the firm had a brief period of success.

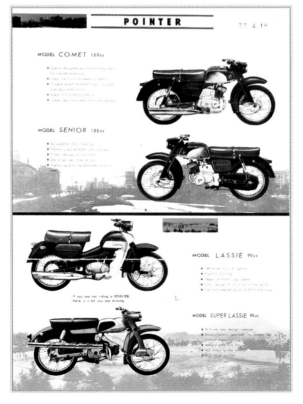

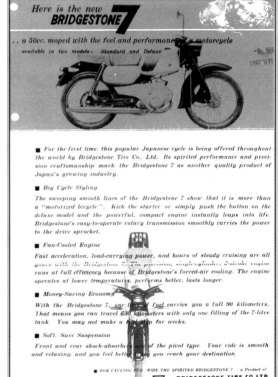

It was 1956 when the next step was taken. The engineers got hold of the most advanced production two-stroke of the era, the Adler MB 250. Adler was to stop making motorcycles one year later, for reasons unconnected with quality problems. Production was too expensive. People did not appreciate the standard of quality enough to be willing to pay the high retail price. Perhaps in fact the Adler was too good. Whatever, the 16 bhp machine was a very good example for Yamaha to follow, with the YD 1.

Now Yamaha engineers became more self-confident. They pleaded to be allowed to design their own chassis, claiming they could make a frame that would be cheaper to build and yet would be at least

equal to the Adler's; possibly better. The clinching argument was that the home-made frame would be far more modern.

They were given the go-ahead.

So the 1956 YD 1 had a very Adler-like engine and an all-Yamaha frame. This great emphasis on quality, already on view in Mr. Honda's products, put Yamaha on the map in spite of the cut-throat battle that was going on in the industry at that time. The YD 1 can, with respect to quality, be compared to the 1955 SA and SB Dream singles of Honda. Both Honda and Yamaha models underwent continuous improvement and the 1960 YD 2 became a rival for the by then famous C 71 Dream produced by Honda.

The YD 2 was the first Yamaha the Western world saw. Like the Honda SA, the Yamaha YD 2 was a good machine; however its performance, if no worse, was no better than that of the European opposition.

Now Yamaha history splits into two versions. In Europe it started in 1961 in Holland; it was a failure. Yamaha would later make a come-back with the YDS 3. (This will be described in the chapter dealing with the 1960s.) In Japan things were different. Yamaha was convinced that racing was good for development. The very first Yamaha, the 125 YA 1, was immediately entered in the now regularly held Asama races; and it won. The YD 1, however, was not a winner: the 16 in wheels were a disadvantage; the pressed-steel frame was too heavy for racing; the entire bike just wasn't advanced enough.

Back to the drawing board! A Norton Featherbed frame was perhaps not precisely copied, but some

Yamaha YA 3 of 1961: a little further ahead in development than other two-stroke models, but only just. The YA 3s were good enough to enable Yamaha to survive, however.

This was the way to express speed in the early sixties. It is dangerous and feels unstable (I tried it). From an aerodynamics point of view it is successful, however; you do reach a higher top speed.

Specification	Model YD-2		Engine . . . . YD-2 2 Stroke Engine	
	Overall Length . . . . 1900 mm (74.8″)		Cooling . . . . Air-Cooling	
	Overall Height . . . . 955 mm (37.6″)		Cylinder . . . . 2 Cylinder System	
	Overall Width . . . . 740 mm (29.1″)		Bore and Stroke . 54 mm × 54 mm (2.1″ × 2.1″)	
	Wheelbase . . . . 1270 mm (50.0″)		Cylinder Capacity . . . . . 247 c.c. 15 cu. in.	
Yamaha	Net Weight . . . . 140 kg (309 lbs.)		Compression Ratio . . . . 1 : 6.6	
	Maximum Speed . . . . . 115 km/h (71 m.p.h.)		Ignition System . . . . Battery Ignition	
	Climbing Ability . . . . ⅕		Carburetor . . . . . . Model: AMAL VM 20 1T	
	Brake Efficiency . 10.5 m/50 km/h (34′/31 m.p.h.)		Clutch . . . . Multi-Plate Clutch	
	Brakes . . . . front: Drum Type, Hand Brake		Transmission . Foot-Operated 4 Speed Gear-Box	
	rear: Drum Type, Foot Brake		and Chain	
	Tires . . . . front: 3.25″ × 16″, 4-ply		Transmission Ratio	
	rear: 3.25″ × 16″, 4-ply		Low 1 : 25.601 3rd 1 : 10.917	
	Suspension System . front: Telescopic Oil-Damper		2nd 1 : 14.631 Top 1 : 8.420	
	rear: Swing Arm Oil-Damper		Fuel Consumption . . . . 35 km/l (80 mile/gallon)	
	Fuel Tank Capacity . . . . . . 13 l (3.5 gallon)		Motor Oil Mixing Ratio . . . . 20 : 1	
	Starting System . . . . Starter Dynamo			

The first attempt to export Yamaha 250cc YD 2s failed. Only 20 were sold in Europe. The Adler is still recognisable in the engine.

lines of the new Yamaha racing frame can be traced back to Rex McCandless's Featherbed design. The 1957 250 cc Asama racer from Yamaha had been a hit, and the production 1958 Yamaha YDS 1 had 18 in wheels and a frame of steel tube, like the racer. The single carburettor of the YD 1 was changed for a pair on the first YDS. (S stood for Sports.) The YDS series was developed parallel to the YDs, which were more and more focused on a touring rôle. We will see a similar development with the Dream and CB models of Honda. Only a few examples of the YDS 1 were exported, some reaching Australia and the USA, where they became the basis for a successful sportsbike. So in Japan at this stage it could be said that Yamaha might be considered to be slightly ahead of Honda, as far as production sportsters were concerned. On the racetrack and in the markets of the rest of the world, however, it was very much the other way round.

■ ▩ Colleda/Suzuki ▩ ■

Suzuki was an old and established manufacturer of wooden weaving looms, and also distributed cotton – a logical thing to do, for it kept demand for looms

alive in pre-war agricultural Japan. In 1952, when Japan entered a new era with regained independence, there was surplus capacity in the factory, so the decision was taken to manufacture engines that could be clipped to a bicycle. One of the first engines was the Power Free, a worthy rival to Honda's A model and the Cub. In the early fifties little four-stroke engines were made for SJK Cox motorcycles. Suzuki did not make motorcycles, they made these engines which were sold to other manufacturers.

Around the same time as Yamaha, Suzuki started developing their own motorcycle. They, too, got hold of an Adler, and studied it well. Shunzo Suzuki decided that their motorcycles should not be made under the name of the loom company. So they were not called Suzuki, but Colleda. The reasoning behind this was that if the motorcycle department was to fail, the good name of Suzuki would not be damaged; motorcycles, after all, were not the main product of the company.

The first Colleda was comparable with the Yamaha YD 1 in that the engine was very Adler-like; but the cycle parts were very 'Colleda'. Styling was very outspoken, with the huge headlight. The Colleda TT of 1956 was a remarkable machine. Oriental eyes loved the styling though a Westerner would probably react quite differently. The enormous headlight looks like a horseshoe from the front; it would become a Colleda trademark. Like Yamaha, the model developed as time passed. The Colleda was adapted more and more to the tastes of the US and European public, because the export market was the goal. The 1959 Colleda Twin Ace (TA), only a few years after the TT, was a beauty. The styling studies had resulted in a very specific Colleda outline, rather 'Jet Age' …. Sharp edges and carefully chosen lines. Aeroplanes such as the De Havilland Comet and the French Caravelle were sources of inspiration. In Japan a leading-link front fork and 16 in wheels were practical on the unpaved roads and were also considered to be fashionable. Like Honda's C 71 Dream, the Colleda TA was a good bike but it wasn't top of the pile in Western eyes. Where the Honda was technically advanced enough to become successful, anyway, the Colleda didn't make the breakthrough. It did have some unusual features – the hydraulically operated rear brake, for example. Both brakes were coupled and operated by the pedal; 60 % of the pressure to the front an 40 % to the rear wheel. The high quality of finish was another notable point. If you look at a TA closely,

The 1955 SJK model ST 1. The Suzuki loom factory built the engine. As with the first Yamaha Red Dragon of the same year, the influence of the 1949 DKW RT 125 shows through strongly in this model, later to become a Suzuki.

One year after the SJK, ▶ Suzuki used the brand name Colleda. The first 250, the 1956 Colleda TT, had much in common with the Adler MB 250. Styling was very distinctive, but would become more and more "normal" in the next three years.

you will notice that the light-alloy castings are extremely well made. Nothing cheap here; it's pure industrial art.

Successor to the TA was, logically enough, the TB, which was well adapted to 'our' tastes. The TB was followed by the Colleda TC, and then by the T 10; and now the sixties were upon us. The Colleda T 10 was renamed Suzuki T 10 in 1963. Technically speaking, the developments were not enormous. The engines still had a clear resemblance to the Adler from which they were derived. Adler had successfully overcome seizure problems but Colledas seized frequently, a problem which would only be resolved with the T 20, fitted with alloy cylinders. The crankcases of a Colleda split horizontally, contrary to Adler's vertical split, offering a far stronger setup. Development had already started on the Colleda. An attempt to export to Britain failed. Some machines made it to Belgium and the UK, but in total no great quantities were exported.

Suzuki made a big splash, in 1966, with the all new T 20. In the 125 cc department Colleda also started with a DKW copy, in 1955. Like the Yamaha YA 1, the Colleda 125 single was very much a DKW RT 125. In 1959, however, the successor was a beautiful twin-cylinder model. Technically speaking, we are dealing with a shrunken Adler here. The Colleda 125 Seltwin, as it was named, was the first

motorcycle to bear the S logo on the fuel tank – the first sign that Colleda was going to make it. Shunzo Suzuki was now so confident that he permitted motorcycles to carry the Suzuki name. The few Twin Aces that reached Europe had Suzuki logos. They were, of course, re-labelled Colledas. The last of the Colleda line, the Colleda T 10, was officially the first of the new make by the name of Suzuki and became the 1963 250 cc Suzuki T 10.

■ BACK TO HONDA ■
ONE MAN SHAPES HISTORY

Soichiro Honda led all the Japanese makers. He deserves this separate chapter. We have seen that between 1951 and 1955 dozens of makers produced simple motorcycles of relatively poor quality. It was a seller's market; nobody (with a few exceptions) bothered about improving the product. But after 1955 people began to look out for quality. Honda foresaw that this would happen as early as 1953. He knew, better than anybody, that his products were not good enough when stacked up against the best non-Japanese makes. First, he had to deal with a cash shortage. He succeeded in convincing his workers that the financial problems of the company could only be overcome if they were prepared to work a few months without payment! No force, no threats; openness and dialogue did the job. The people agreed, and so the banks granted Honda a

Major breakthrough: ▶ the 1956 Honda C 70 Dream (250 cc) was a completely new model that owed nothing to any European make or model. This was the first true Honda, and signalled the start of the great success that Soichiro Honda would go on to enjoy.

The new face of Colleda in 1959, showing 'Jet-age' styling. This Colleda Seltwin was a 150 cc model. Although there were 'S' logos on the tank and the sidecover said 'Suzuki', the machine was marketed as a Colleda.

loan. The company was saved.

Honda's next step was, for a Japanese, very, very unorthodox: he went to Europe on a study trip. No businessman ever set foot outside Japan in those days. Honda decided that he needed to understand what made a Triumph, or an NSU, or a Norton so successful. Where better to turn to than the factory concerned? Honda visited Edward Turner in England. Turner was impressed by the attitude of the little Japanese businessman; he realised his visitor was something special, but he did not appreciate the implications of Honda's mission. Honda was like a sponge; he absorbed all he could learn. He visited the TT races in the Isle of Man. He was impressed by the performance of European motorcycles. Then he went to DAF in Holland who had very innovative ideas about production methods. He went to Germany to NSU, where he was tremendously impressed by the 250 Rennmax and the NSU racing team. Horex was another make Honda regarded highly. Then on to Kreidler where he was overwhelmed by the modern and efficient way Kreidler's mopeds were produced. He was astounded at the fine engineering tolerances achieved on the production lines. All these manufacturers were happy to explain to the little man from Japan the how and why of their

production techniques; in short they told him everything he wanted to know. Honda absorbed it all.

Back in Japan, Honda realised that he had to start at the very roots of the motorcycle production process if he wanted to attain the quality he was after. Bear in mind that in 1954 there was still a seller's market; there was no reason at that time, apparently, to look for improvements in quality. Honda found there was no Japanese milling machine that could perform precisely enough to meet his new-found standards.

The 305 cc Honda C 75 in 1956, from an original black and white photograph heavily worked on and coloured by the factory artist.

Factory shot of C 71 engines on the test bed. Each engine was run before it was installed in a motorcycle.

見学者通路

Study in styling: 250 cc 1960 CE 71 with 18 in wheels. A few dozen were built. Styling resembled the 125 cc CB 92 Benly Super Sports. With the birth of the 250 cc CB 72 this model was rapidly abandoned.

It was considered very disloyal to buy machinery outside Japan other than for study purposes. Now Honda wanted to buy complete production plants from 'the barbarians'. In the end he succeeded in getting permission, and financing as well. For more than 1 million dollars he bought American, Swiss and German machinery. Now he had the tools to fulfil his dreams.

Honda believed that he would build better motorcycles when he did not merely copy European examples, but added his own improvements. The first model of this 'new generation' was the JA 125 Benly. Benly means 'convenient, satisfactory'. It was clearly influenced by the NSU Fox. The Benly was a good machine, but no better than the NSU. By contemporary Japanese standards, it was excellent. Honda was not satisfied, although none of his peers understood why: the bike was good; so what was the problem?

The next model Honda made was another step forward: this was the SA 250 Dream single. The engine was based on the Horex Regina but was housed in a frame designed by Honda, with clear Horex influence. The Regina was a pushrod engine, but the Honda was an overhead-cam design. Honda was moving away from straight cloning. The SA 250 was of outstanding quality. So was the SB 350, as well as the ME and MF, their successors. But still Honda was not satisfied, and again nobody could understand why. Honda wanted not merely to match the quality of the European machines, but to beat them. And he wanted his bikes to perform better. Already, he was first among Japanese; but his bikes were still not a match for the Europeans.

Honda went to the drawing board to design his first 'original' motorcycle. It was 1956, and the C 70 Dream was the result. Horex influence? NSU influence? Take all the bikes, put them next to each other, and see the differences. Honda's 250 cc ohc twin cylinder had 20 bhp on tap. Anybody could ride it; anybody could buy it. And it was reliable. These were new standards of excellence. Development did not stop. In 1958 an electric starter was added, when the model was titled C 71 Dream.

This is, historically, a very important motorcycle, in being the first Japanese bike to be sold outside Japan. In 1959 144 C 71s found their way to Holland, and 205 went to Britain. A couple of hundred were sold in the USA (although some sources claim that the number sold was as low as 69). The next Honda model was of 50 cc, signalling the birth of the C 100 Super Cub. The year of introduction was 1958, and it was the start of Honda's conquest of the world market (although, as

noted, the C 71 Dream was the first Honda to be marketed outside Japan). The entire production of Super Cubs in 1958 and 1959 was sold in Japan. In 1960 the C 100 appeared on the world market, having dominated the home market over the previous two years. Even today, we see this model and its descendants literally all over the world. It was the two-wheeled equivalent of Henry Ford's Model T. Then in 1959 the third important model came off the drawing board, the 125cc C 92 Benly, together

The old factory stands for the huge European motorcycle industry of the fifties and sixties; the 1959 Honda C 71 Dream, having changed the face of motorcycling, is shown as a monument itself.

Sales brochure of 1959. For the American market Honda offered a Scrambler version of the Dream. Virtually all later machines would follow the example of this model.

with its high-performance brother, the CB 92 Benly Super Sports. This was – is – again a miracle of a motorcycle!

■ ▨ Racing ▨ ■

Motorcycles have been raced in Europe since their creation. The drive behind racing is simple: it improves the breed. In Japan there was some primitive racing of a kind in pre-war days. The bikes were all of European origin. British machines such as Nortons and Velocettes found their way to Japan, although never in great numbers. It was around 1953 that racing of some importance began. The first races could fairly be classified as 'all-Japanese'. The import of European or American motorcycles was not forbidden, but rules made it very, very difficult. In fact, these were not real races but, in the main, hillclimb competitions, only gradually evolving into races, at Mount Asama.

Initially, standard machines were used. The first real race was won by a SY Lilac single, in the 250cc class. Meguros were there, close to the front. The first 125 race was won by a Yamaha YA 1. Colleda completely missed out on racing in those days. Yamaha built a racing version of the YD 1 and secured a class win in 1957. Honda had set up a study to produce a racing bike: it was to be a 250 four-cylinder four-stroke, with single overhead camshaft, driven by bevel gear from the crankshaft. The spindly frame with flimsy front forks made its looks rather a joke. It showed up at Asama in 1958, and won first time out! Yamaha

and Honda, it seemed, were on the brink of a real battle both on the track and in the market place. Then in 1959 a Honda GP team arrived in the Isle of Man. They were going to compete in the Lightweight TT. The Hondas, dohc 125 twins, were impressive, but the team had forgotten that in Europe races took place on tarmac; not on gravel! Nonetheless, all six bikes entered finished in the top ten, winning the team award.

■ ▨ Shake-out ▨ ■

We have seen that by the second half of the 1950s only a few among the dozens of marques originally in the market remained. Some manufacturers simply went bankrupt, others merged. And of course there were some firms that decided they should not be in the motorcycle business, and changed their product line. We all know of Fuji films; but who remembers, or even knows, that there have been Fuji motorcycles? Mitsubishi is a financial institute and is a well established car maker. Once, they made

Piston and valves of the 50cc DOHC Honda CR 110 production racer.

◄ Honda's Dream was not to be alone for long. Here are a 1966 Suzuki T 20, a 1964 Honda CB 72 and a 1968 Kawasaki A 7 Avenger, with the 1959 Honda C 71.

scooters by the name of Pigeon and Silver Pigeon. Scooters … or should we say two-wheeled trucks? Showa is still in business as a manufacturer of front forks and shock absorbers. They used to make motorcycles. Pointer now only make pedal cycles. Once you could have put a 1962 Pointer 125 next to a 1962 Honda 125, and have seen the cross-

fertilisation. But the Pointer, although well built, was conventional, and on its way to oblivion. By 1964 it was all over. Not even the 125 twin-cylinder Pointer racer could change things. Honda set new standards; it's clear that the company was on its way to the top. Meihatsu and Meguro would live on, not with their own names, but under the Kawasaki banner.

Six marques stood a good chance of making it in the late 50s. Today there are four. Kawasaki entered the sixties as the inheritor of Meguro and Meihatsu. Honda is, in fact, the only survivor among the early marques. This is thanks to Soichiro Honda's vision. He fully deserved his honour of being the first foreigner to be granted a place in America's Hall of Fame. Suzuki and Yamaha were relative newcomers. So was Bridgestone, and it was too late for them.

The first Colleda to go abroad was this 1960 250cc Twin Ace. A dozen or so were exported to Belgium. Jet Age styling, however, was not the right choice for Western countries. Technically, the interesting features were the hydraulically operated brakes, coupled by the rear brake pedal. An extra cable provided for separate operation of the front brake.

◄ Restored 1960 Honda C 76 Dream. This is the 305 cc version of the C 71. It did not have extensions under the emblems on the fuel tank. It was superseded by the C 77.

They were headed for success, but when it became evident that the others had become so strong, dictating the market, Bridgestone stopped production, in 1969.

The last candidate to make it into the sixties was in fact given a place in the market by the others. Lilac was the second 'old' manufacturer. Misfortunes in the technical department prevented Lilac being a success; 1967 was the last year any significant numbers of Lilac (or rather, Marusho) motorcycles were produced.

FOCUS ON THE HONDA C71 ■ ■ DREAM ■ ■

Nineteen-fifty-nine was a memorable year. Amsterdam had a world scoop when the RAI motorcycle show, held in January that year, gave the Western world a glimpse of the first motorcycle to be officially exported from Japan. It was the 250cc twin-cylinder Honda C 71 Dream. This name had been used before: a prototype Brough Superior was called the Dream, in 1939. Soichiro Honda had dreams – a vision – about mass transport throughout the world. He, a humble little Japanese, was going to provide cheap transport for everybody. Many models to come would carry the Dream name. Example: a CB 400 N was known from 1980 officially by the factory as a Super Dream CB 400 N. Nobody uses the name any more; but that is the background.

It was September 1957 when the first 250 twin was sold in Japan. The previous model, the SA single, also having the name of Dream, was still being built at that time. The new twin was far better than the single, and soon the latter was phased out in favour of the all-new design. Horizontally split crankcases contain a four-bearing crankshaft driving an overhead camshaft via a chain. Light-alloy pistons run in a light-alloy cylinder barrel having cast-iron liners, and the camshaft runs in ball bearings in the light-alloy cylinder head. There are two valves per cylinder. A reliable 6 volt generator sits on the right of the crankshaft, also driving the contact-breaker, with current to a distributor cap situated at the end of the camshaft, on the cylinder head. In 1956 only racing bikes had such a sophisticated specification and racing bikes were not available to the average motorcyclist. But this Honda was a production bike which could be bought by anyone.

The clutch is at the other end of the crankshaft, driving the four-speed gearbox via a single chain. Lubrication is well looked after in the new Honda. The dry sump system is fed by a powerful oil pump. Engine and gearbox are built as one unit. The frame is made of steel pressings, as are the front forks. The styling was a great success, by Japanese standards. Leading link forks and 16in wheels were very fashionable, and not only in Japan. They performed well on the poor roads of the 1950s. Telescopic forks already existed but they were not as efficient as they became later on. On bumpy roads a leading link was more comfortable. Note that one of the early devotees of telescopic front forks, BMW, began to use an Earles fork in the late fifties. The C 70 had 20 bhp on tap, when rivals could not better 14 or 16. Top speed was high for the time, at 135kph. It may be

The 1959 Honda C 71 Dream, a sporting machine in its day. Every component was neatly made and worked well. This, together with the right performance and durability, ensured the breakthrough of Honda. Other makers had to wait years before they could match the quality of this model. (See also top of page 28)

hard to believe today, but in those days this Honda as considered to be a fast, sporty bike. One of the best sports bike of the era, the Adler MB 250, was not as fast as a Dream – though the Adler's handling was superior. The C 75, the 305cc version of the C 70, appeared a few months later, and was faster still. The detail finish of these new Dreams was as good as the engine. Large full-width hubs with good brakes were not usual in 1956; winkers as a standard feature weren't, either. Lighting was good for the period, something that could not be said of many bikes in those days.

In late 1958 the model got an electric starter. Now the model was called the C 71. Even during production, improvements continued. Late in 1959 the spark distributor made way for a double coil, to improve ignition timing. It was immediately put into production; no waiting for the new model year. Early C 71s have a gearbox that can be shifted directly from top into first by schifting up agian. This was a popular feature in Japan. The Japanese like to sprint into top gear, to the next traffic light, and then brake without downshifting. Having come to a halt in top gear, it is easy to shift once more and end up ready for the next take off in first. Not so the European rider. He wants to be sure he is in top gear and does not count gears, as a Japanese apparently does. A Western rider who isn't sure if he is in top could have a surprise if the cracking and rattling indicates that he is trying for first gear at 100kph …. The gearbox forces selection of fourth gear in such a situation, and it is this top gear that doesn't survive the violent treatment and breaks down. Later examples of the C 71 have a normal return-shift gearbox; Honda listened to his customers. The end of 1959 was when the 305cc version of the C 71, known as the C 76, saw light of day. This version also went to Europe.

■ ▨ Testing ▨ ■

The first tests were a cause for celebration. Gerhard Klomps, who had literally been waiting outside the RAI building all night, was the first Western journalist to ride the C 71. The morning before the RAI motorcycle show, he rode the only example in Europe. He was excited about the bike, believing it to have the makings of a challenge to established Western manufacturers. Dealers and motorcyclists were more cautious than the press, but very soon the new Honda machines found their way out to the public. In Holland there was no real resistance. In Britain the home manufacturers were soon

threatening motorcycles dealers with the sack were they to sell Hondas. If they sold Hondas, they would not be allowed to market Triumphs or Nortons. Soon some dealers said they didn't care: they were going to stock Hondas! When Honda began importing to other European countries, the barriers were crumbling and sales were firm from the start. The USA's reaction to the C 71 was 'moderate'. This was not the bike they were waiting for; the C 100 would turn out to be that one…

■ ▩ Touring ▩ ■

The riding public had mixed feelings about the C 71. They loved the engine, and its power. The C 71 was raced in standard classes; there had been reports of Dreams beating 175 Ducatis. A Ducati handled far better than the Honda, but the Dream was faster. If only the engine could be fitted in a real sportbike .... That is exactly what happened in 1960 when the C 71 Dream was transformed into the C 72, and then this vastly improved Dream got a sporting brother, the CB 72 Super Sports. In the USA it was known as the Hawk. The Dream was left to fill a rôle as a modern touring bike. The C 72 carried lubricant in the engine, making the system semi-wet sump. Gone was the oil tank on the righthand side. The clutch moved to the mainshaft. It was easier in operation and became totally reliable. The transmission shafts were now fixed in the crankcase.

During production of the C 72, Honda found it necessary to change the position of the oil passages in the cylinder barrel. If a modified cylinder was placed on the unmodified crankcase, no oil would reach the camshaft. The camshaft was changed, too. The one-piece C 71 item was superseded by twin camshafts joined together by the sprocket, which also served as drive for the ignition advance, through the hollow right camshaft. On some examples it was enlarged to become a counterbalance weight. Not all C 72s have this feature: those that do, vibrate less. I am referring here to examples with a 360-degree crankshaft. Almost all Dreams are 360-degree machines and almost all CB 72 Super Sports have a 180-degree crank. The converse does occur, however. All this demonstrates that the learning process for Honda was going on even during production. Yamaha went through a similar phase at this time with the YDS 3 and the YDS 5 range. The same sort of development can be seen in the cycle parts. Winkers change, grow bigger. Construction of the pressed-steel handlebar is altered. After 1964 the handlebar becomes tubular, more to American tastes. 1964 is also the year when the chopping and changing comes to an end for Honda. The C 72, the

C 77 (1963 successor to the C 76), the CB 72 and the CB 77 (305cc Super Hawk) now share almost every construction detail. The C keeps its 360° crank and the CB the 180° crank, but it is possible to interchange engine internals.

The model has matured. It will remain virtually unchanged till the end of production, in 1967. The last Dreams were sold in 1968. In the 1990s restoring a Dream is not an easy task. When it was in production, parts were a problem. These days you have to sort out the series you're dealing with. What cylinder block, what crankshaft, what camshaft, what piston? Does the engine belong to the frame? Example: an early C 72 engine will fit in a late CB 77 frame, and vice versa. Is the year correct? You have to have the right answers.

In the sixties the learning process was not restricted (only) to the design department. Delivery of parts was not easy. The most famous example of that is exhausts. Importers would find they only had – for instance – leftside mufflers. When ordering right ones they'd get left ones, again and again! And of course the other way round. Nowadays, I have to say, the parts position seems to be better than in the Dream's production days. Getting the parts is not the biggest problem, provided you can accept the modern level of prices. This goes for the C 72 and C 77. The early models, the C 71 and C 76, are a different story. There are no parts! You need a specialist to get the right advice. Dreams are tough machines. Many of them will have served their owner(s) for more than 20 years before breaking down. But when they do give trouble, you'll find a lot of wear.

A restored Dream enjoys only low value these days, which is rather unfair. Historically, it is a very important machine. After all, it opened the modern era in motorcycling, nothing less. The day will come when this will be recognised. There aren't many Dreams left. Those that are will take some work before they can be ridden and shown in a concours. If you have one, you have a truly exclusive motorcycle.

THE ROARING SIXTIES

60 STORMY DEVELOPMENTS

◀ **Even after the arrival of the Hawk and the Super Hawk (305cc CB 77) the Dream retained its popularity. Shown here is a 1966 C 77 with latest styling. A wide tubular touring handlebar has replaced the previous pressed steel item. The winkers and tail light have been enlarged.**

Honda C 72 (and C 77) carried oil in the engine, as opposed to the C 71 (and C 76), with dry sump lubrication system. The new arrangement made for cleaner lines of the machine.

The sixties was a decade in which many ideas changed throughout society. Pop music broke through in Europe. The USA was ahead of the old world, but Europe was in a ferment too. Think of the Everly Brothers, the Beatles, or, even worse(!), the Rolling Stones. Popularity of this kind of music may be seen as an early sign of prosperity. After reconstruction time following World War Two, we finally had time to think about our way of life and the values that shaped it. Leisure time became important.

All this had big consequences for motorcycling and motorcycles. Europeans were leaving their mopeds and simple motorcycles behind and could, for the first time, buy a little car for the daily trip to work. VW Beetles, Minis, Citroën 2 CVs and Fiat 600s spring to mind. If you could not afford a car, you could at least keep yourself fairly dry on a scooter such as a Vespa or Heinkel. The rôle of motorcycles as a cheap and reliable means of transport was vanishing. Now motorcycling was about fun, thrills. There was logic in this. Motorcycles were not terribly reliable before 1960. Riding one meant getting your hands dirty, regularly. You had to be something of a technician to ride a bike! Here it was Honda (again)

that forced a major breakthrough. This time Europe was ahead of the USA. In Europe riding a motorcycle was more accepted in society than in America. Only criminals and people on the edge of society rode motorcycles in the USA. Honda emphasised that from now on *Everybody* could ride a motorcycle. The old stereotype of a motorcyclist was very carefully

avoided in the advertisements. It was the humble 50cc C 100 Super Cub that was the main subject of the ad. campaigns. It wasn't a macho bike; on the contrary, the advertisements showed people riding C 100s who were accepted members of society, such as housewives, doctors. The slogan was: 'You meet the nicest people on a Honda'. It was this classic campaign and this bike that changed the entire attitude of a nation towards motorcycling in general. Permanently.

One of the important factors was that the advertisements appeared in magazines having nothing to do with motorcycles. Decent people were faced with the phenomenon of motorcycling in their own environment. It was stressed that you wouldn't need tools. These Hondas were as reliable as cars. A C 100 virtually never broke down. Mind you, the message of the advertisements was not altogether new. Harley-Davidson had had a simular style of

advertisement for their 125cc Hummer motorcycle. Even today, this old advertisement is used to highlight the potential of advertising as a marketing tool. The fact that Elvis Presley said something like: "I'm gonna buy me one of those Hondas" (referring to a CB 72) in one of his popular films, of course helped as well. The word 'Honda' became synonymous with 'motorcycle', for a period. The big Kawasaki ship and aircraft building company forced two struggling motorcycle marques owned by them to join forces. Meihatsu and Meguro lost their identity in 1962; from then on they were to use the name of the big company as their trademark, and Kawasaki motorcycles were born. The models were the same as before. Even the logos used had a strong resemblance to 'Meihatsu' and 'Meguro' designs.

They were not sold outside Japan. Very little is known about this period. Kawasaki really started up

The 1961 Yamaha YD 2 still had a lot of the Adler about it. Like Colleda's, this attempt by Yamaha to come up with a competitor for the Honda Dream failed. The Yamaha, earlier than the Suzuki T 10, was slightly more advanced than the also Adler-based Suzuki.

in 1965, when they tried to conquer the US market. The Meguro 650 will be re-christened Kawasaki W 1 and fail to make any real impact, looking too much like a BSA; as did the Meguro. Meihatsus don't make it outside Japan, not even in Kawasaki form. It is only the clout of the mother company that enabled the marque to survive the late fifties and early sixties. Suzuki made it into the sixties under its own steam. Not so brilliant as Honda, they still built little machines, like the U 50, that were really good. The 80, 125 and 250cc bikes were modern enough, just, to make survival a possibility. Not yet a commercial success, Suzuki was nevertheless granted a place in the market.

Suzuki, as noted, used to market their motorcycles as Colledas. By 1963 they were so confident that the Colleda T 10 was re-christened Suzuki T 10. Any bike that went outside Japan was labelled Suzuki, even the one-offs, such as the few Twin Aces that reached Europe. In Japan they were Colleda Twin Aces; we in Europe know them as Suzukis, with an S on the fuel tank. (In Belgium four have surfaced, and I am the lucky owner of one of them). It was the successor to the T 10 that put Suzuki on the map. The T 20 is the first 'real' Suzuki. It was probably designed in 1963, but we first met it in Britain in 1965; the rest of the world saw it in 1966.

In the early sixties the Japanese kept to the small capacity classes, the mainstream bikes being 50 and 125cc. The market for the big machines, in those days 600 and 650cc, was left to the traditional makers in Britain. The Kawasaki W 1 did not disturb this picture. The fact that a Japanese 250 was as fast as a British 500 did not (yet) have a real effect on the appeal of the big bikes. In fact in the early sixties the British even benefited from the Japanese incursion; but after 1965 Britain's manufacturers faced their final decline.

Suzuki and Kawasaki joined in. Bridgestone and Lilac left the battlefield. The four remaining makes took over the market. The Japanese also brought out bigger machines: 350 and 450cc models appeared, followed by true 500s. The market for motorcycles began to grow, albeit slowly. The non-Japanese marques did not reap any benefit from this, however; BMW, Moto Guzzi and Laverda did, perhaps, to an extent, but they were exceptions, and we are not talking about big numbers here. For BMW, the 1969 R75/5 would open a new life for the Bavarian company. When the end of the decade announced the start of the Superbike era, the European competition was in fact almost non-

existent. Harley Davidson too had big problems. By 1970, Japanese supremacy had been established firmly, all over the world.

HONDA CB 72 SUPERSPORTS
▨ ▨ THE REAL BREAKTHROUGH ▨ ▨

At the end of 1960 the CB 72 was announced to the public. This is the official year of introduction, as registered in history. But I have personally seen a (very scruffy) CB 72 that was built in 1959. In those years the frame and engine numbers indicated the year of construction. This system was abandoned in 1960. Recently found literature indicates even a CB 71 must have existed. That is believed to be early 1959. Many countries didn't see their first CB 72s

A 1959 prototype of the Honda CB 92 Benly Super Sports. It was not marketed in quite this form; look at the front mudguard...

The same can be said about this prototype of the Honda CB 72 Hawk. Production models were to have side covers and separate fuel tank covers instead of a chromed and painted tank.

The 1964 Suzuki T 10. Colleda found that the Twin Ace was not appreciated, so they restyled the machine to Western tastes. This was the first model to be marketed as a Suzuki. Still no success; only a few were sold.

until 1961. This model, the sporty version of the C 72 Dream, was a dream come true. Everything the Dream lacked, the Hawk, as the US came to know this new sports bike, possessed: the wheels were 18in and there was a slim, tubular frame. The bike had an ecstatic reception. Here was a racing bike for sale over the counter! The use of the engine as a stressed member of the chassis had been seen before, but not in such a powerful and modern machine. People just could not believe that this bike could run at almost 10,000rpm and not explode. An overhead camshaft as a standard feature was unbelievable in 1960. Twin carburettors were another mouth-watering feature; yet the bike would happily tickover at low rpm. A 250cc twin cylinder that could run at 90mph and still be reliable was

something dreams were made of in those days. That it actually existed took some time for people to comprehend. Huge duplex brakes not even seen on racing bikes were the next surprise.

In order to emphasise that we were dealing with a genuine streetbike, the Hawk was equipped with a starter motor. You could order traffic indicators, as optional extras. Many companies did not even consider offering this luxury. In 1963 came a 305cc model, CB 77 Supersports, a Super Hawk, almost exactly the same motorcycle as the CB 72 Hawk, but with 55cc more capacity. Only the figures on the tank badge reveal the difference. The model went through the same technical development as the C 72 and C 77 Dreams. The shape and the looks of the model do not really change. In 1964 the steel sliders

The machine that had all the right answers: Honda's CB 72. This is a 1964 model, but the CB 72 Super Sports, or Hawk, was introduced in 1960. It was so advanced that it took other manufacturers six years to match this model.

Special features proliferated on the CB 72. Speedometer and rev-counter in one instrument would become typical of sixties styling. Duplex rear brake was so powerful that even the later Black Bomber would not get it. If you didn't use the electric starter, the kickstarter had to be operated, in a forward direction – very strange! Performance of this two-fifty was still formidable in the 1990s.

of the front fork are replaced by alloy sliders and the lugs of the frame and swinging arm by welded components. One has to look carefully to notice these changes. The rev-counter and the speedo needles go clockwise and anti-clockwise respectively; at full throttle in top gear the needles indicate instantly what the rider wants to know. After 1964, they operate parallel to each other. These are tiny details. Not really important.

A CB 77 was fast enough to challenge a Triumph Daytona, a BMW R 69 S or a Norton Atlas. In fact, for *Das Motorrad's* reporter, Ernst Leverkus, 'Klacks' to his friends, the Super Hawk was the fastest bike he ever took around the Nürbergring. *Das Motorrad* used to make a point of these speed tests on the circuit. The fact that the CB 77 gave a lot of ccs away did not matter. In England there was an advertisement that asked: 'Who will win the cc versus RPM race?' This resulted in uproar. It was considered sacriligious to compare the two bikes illustrated: the picture showed a Honda Supersports with the outline of a Vincent HRD in the background. Vincents stopped production in 1955, but the prestige of these beautiful machines was still very high. However, the message was clear: Honda stood for modern motorcycles of excellent quality.

The last CB 72 left the assembly line in 1967, although there are indications that some were built in January 1968. There have been slightly altered versions, with chrome fenders and folding footrests, exported to Canada and the USA. The CBs 250 and 350 were built according to the construction lines of the CB 450 Black Bomber (which we shall meet later). They perform even better than the CB 72/77 Supersports machines; in fact, they are outstanding motorcycles, but their impact is not half as great as that of the earlier bikes. Times have changed by then. A 250 (or 305) is no longer a major class on the eve of the Superbike era. The 350s of the other manufacturers are at the least as good as the CB 350.

HONDA CB92 BENLY SUPER SPORTS
▩ ▩ A GEM INDEED ▩ ▩

A 125cc motorcycle was considered after the war in Europe as nothing more than a cheap form of transport. In the USA, with the automobile already commonplace, the market for small-capacity machines was very small. It's easy to understand why the 125cc Harley Hummer never made it. But Europeans rode to work on these little machines. They had to be reliable and easy to handle. Examples of machines that performed this task were the DKW RT 125 and its derivative, the BSA Bantam.

When Honda followed up on the Dream and brought out the C 92 and CB 92, reactions differed significantly. The C 92 can be seen as a 125cc clone of a Dream, when it did not receive much attention. Of course, it was an excellent motorcycle, but everyone took that for granted by then. And, yes, it was a success, less so than the Dream, but still a success. Now commuters were offered a 125 twin-cylinder four-stroke with an electric starter. It was almost luxurious, and certainly relatively expensive. It was not a replacement for the Bantam, for that role was earmarked for the C 100 Super Cub. The CB 92, 125 counterpart of the CB 72, was something quite different. The press were delighted. Again they could not find enough superlatives to describe Mr Honda's advanced technology. It would be decades before such 125 exotica would be seen again. It was closer to the touring C 92 than the CB 72 was to the Dream, but in order to make it a sportsbike Honda went even further than with the Hawk. The Benly Super Sports retained a pressed-steel frame and forks. The rear section was made

slimmer, and unshrouded rear shocks replaced the square suspension units of the touring bike; 18in wheels replaced the 16in wheels of the C 92. The hubs were worthy of a factory racer: superior magnesium drum of large diameter gave the Benly outstanding stopping power. In fact, they were similar to the brakes used in production racers. And all this at a time when buying a racer was akin to buying a Space Shuttle for private purposes! The entire finish of the CB 92 made the bike look very much like a factory racer. The slim front guard that moved with the wheel, the little fairing for the headlamp, the racer-like fuel tank – it was all there. The sound, as well.

But this 'racer' could be started with an electric motor. It was, after all, a streetbike. Performance lived up to expectations. The overhead-cam engine happily went over the 10,000rpm red line. At the other extreme, tickover at a few hundred rpm was absolutely reliable. Just like the CB 72, it signalled a stunning advance of standards in motorcycle construction.

Commercially, the Benly Super Sports is not an important bike. Historically, it is one of the true milestones. The retail cost of a CB 92 would almost buy a 250cc C 72 Dream, for it was twice the price of other 125s. There was no '125 culture' other than the ride-to-work machines. A C 100 would perform that duty perfectly; so there was no market for this little racing gem. The people who did buy them went to the circuits to race the bikes. Honda could provide a full racing kit. Honda's pre-eminence would last until 1968 when the Yamaha AS 1 took over the Benly's racing position. In 1965 the CB 92 is

Sales brochure of 125 cc models from Honda around 1960. Touring C 92 is next to the 'jewel' of the range, the CB 92 sportster.

Benly Super Sport was ▶ very expensive, so was bought mainly for racing. Relatively few were sold because only a little more money would buy you a 250cc Dream.

superseded by the CB 93. This bike is a detailed clone of the CB 72, but smaller in every respect – yet heavier than the Benly Super Sports. The single carburettor of the CB 92 has been replaced by twin carbs. The magnesium brakes have disappeared.

Now the model is well balanced and everything is 'sensible'. The CB 92 will be renamed CB 125 SS, without model changes other than colours. This is still a beautiful bike but since the CB 72 is already available, it is not particularly exciting. In fact, it is in every respect a better machine than the Benly. It even screams louder and runs faster. I have ridden one at 75mph. Sheer joy! Yet it is the original CB 92 Benly Super Sports that is the true juwel.

It is interesting to compare the CB 92 with, for example, a Pointer 125 Senior of the same year. Pointer is one of those makes that did not survive. When it is compared with the Benly Super Sports, it's clear to see why. My own 1962 Pointer, one of the last made, is very well constructed with carefully designed parts. The single-cylinder two-stroke can be considered to be a much-improved BSA Bantam unit in fact, it would be very useful for commuting. It was put on sale in the USA, but, as stated previously, the Americans were not interested in commuter bikes. In Europe, no Pointer was ever sold. Although there was a market for such bikes, the cheap Honda C 100 did the job perfectly. If you were not into motorcycling but wanted simple transport, the C 100 was the thing to buy. Europeans could still buy the 'real' Bantam. If Pointer had been a European manufacturer, the story might have been quite different. Protectionism was rife in Europe at the time. Pointer did not have any exotic production models to make people proud of owning one. There have been a few racers from Pointer, but they didn't make it to the track.

If I put my Pointer next to my 1962 CB 92, I can see clearly why Pointer is a loser and Honda a winner. Neither was sold in great quantities, yet the CB 92 is the true classic in the 125 line of motorcycles of the post-war era, even though it was not a marketing success.

(left) **Twin-cylinder Benly engine has the clutch on the mainshaft, not on the crank, as on the contemporary Dream. Compare this 1963 engine with any other production 125 of the same age...**

(right) **Full racing technique as displayed in the front wheel of the CB 92, with its magnesium twin leading shoe brake.**

◀ **If a Benly is ridden on full song the exhaust note is even higher than that of a two-stroke. If motorcycle noise is music to your ears, this rates as a chartbuster!**

(below left) **The slim lines of the CB 92. Today, a moped has wider tyres than the Honda.**

(right) **Race-inspired fuel tank was made of aluminium until 1961. Later versions were in steel, and of exactly the same shape and colour as before.**

C 100
▦ ▦ A TWO-WHEELED T FORD ▦ ▦

In Holland, the country that played such a big role in the early history of the Japanese motorcycle industry in Europe, the C 100 Super Cub is very rarely seen. Don't be misled by the figure in the model name; it is a 50cc bike. The Dutch didn't buy anything under 250cc. They commuted on mopeds, when no licence was required. A C 100 was classified as a motorcycle, for which you needed a licence. In the rest of the world, however, this little machine was nothing less than revolutionary. In 1958 and 1959 Japan itself took the entire production of no fewer than 750,000 units. Sales were so strong, you'd think they were being given away. Then came the sales effort in the USA. Americans wouldn't buy the BSA Bantam, but the reliable, clean and easy-to-ride Super Cub was a different matter. People who'd never even thought about riding a motorcycle could now be found on a C 100, running errands. They rode it the first time out as if they had always done so. And enjoyed themselves. "You meet the nicest people on a Honda" made of riding a motorcycle acceptable. The little step-through, as this kind of model was later named, was so easy to ride. The pushrod OHV single has three gears. The clutch is designed so that it disengages automatically when the shift-pedal is moved. The clutch also automatically disengages at tickover. It was designed by Pavel Husak of Jawa in (then) Czechoslovakia. Honda paid handsomely for the design, they certainly didn't steal it. Who told me that? Husak in person, when I showed him such a clutch among my stock!

▪ ▦ Rest of the world ▦ ▪

The conquest of the world market by Honda went on. The C 100 was exported to the Asian countries where it took only a few years to totally change the character of traffic in those far-off lands. The C 100 was a whole new phenomenon. It was the same story in Africa. Even today Super Cubs or successors, such as the ohc C 50, can be seen threading a way through crowded traffic in the countries of the so-called Third World. Millions and millions were sold. In France the little Honda won a 1962 prize for good design. Soichiro Honda was honoured: his product had found recognition in a world that was used to quality; it meant a lot to him that he was recognised in Europe. America, too, added to his glory. He was the first non-American to be awarded a place in the Hall of Fame. He deserved it, for he had given wheels to a great part of the world, like Henry Ford before him.

Other manufacturers have tried to copy the C 100, of course. Yamaha's V 50, Suzuki's U 50; even Kawasaki had something like the Honda. But none came even close to the original. The early Super Cub clones were two-strokes. Later competition changed to four-stroke engines. Yamaha and Suzuki managed to sell their runabouts in considerable numbers, but the sales were minute in comparison to Honda figures. The original C 100 was built until 1967. Then exactly the same concept was followed in the C 50. Only now there was forced lubrication instead of splash lubing. An overhead-camshaft was fitted, and the front forks and headlight were improved. There was more suspension travel. Success continued. In total, more than 15 million C 100 and C 50 machines were sold. And the Cub is still available today. The 1958 design will probably make it into the next century! Though so many C 100 have been built, only a few C 110 Sports Cubs were made. Sources speak of only 11,000. It was meant for the youth of Japan, but it was sold outside Japan as well. Four gears and a manually operated clutch make it different; plus an alloy instead of an iron cylinder head. The-T bone frame got a high exhaust.

YAMAHA
▦ ▦ THE FIRST ATTEMPT ▦ ▦

One year after the Honda CB 72, Yamaha launched an assault on Europe via the Dutch market. In 1961, 20 Yamaha YD 2s were imported into Holland. The Yamaha YD 2 was the fruit of the second round of development, after the Adler-oriented YD 1 of 1956.

The pressed steel frame and the telescopic front fork were well received in 1961. The engine was still very close to the Adler design of 1952. In 1960 it would still have been classified as 'good', if only the Honda CB 72 were not present to point up the difference. But since it was, the Yamaha was considered rather a disappointment. Having been acquainted with the CB 72 for a year, people felt that any new Japanese bike had to beat the Hawk. Or, at the very least, it had to be an equal. The YD 2 was not. Compared to

a Dream, the Yamaha was perhaps slightly more modern, but its quality was not yet as high as the Dream.

But compared with a C 72, the Yamaha was a worthy competitor. The Yamaha YDS 1 would have been more appropriate competition for the CB 72, but very few ever reached the export lines.

In Britain there were of course many Villiers-engined machines, and the BSA Bantam, and Triumph had the 200cc Tiger Cub. The Yamaha was more

You meet the nicest people on a Honda (a C 100 Super Cub of 50 cc). This is still true after 40 years of the C 100; modern variants of the original concept of 1958 are around today.

YOU MEET THE NICEST PEOPLE ON A HONDA

World's Largest Motorcycle Manufacturer
HONDA

In 1960 there was a sports version of the Super Cub, the Sports Cub (C110). The early version had three gears, with manual clutch.

Thanks to this slogan, in 1961 motorcycling became acceptable to society as a whole. The ad campaign is still referred to in marketing schools today.

advanced than these, but not by very much. The Yamaha YD 2, not being such a revolutionary machine as the Honda CB 72, was not generally accepted. After those 20, no more were imported into Europe. Worldwide, the fate of the Yamaha was more or less the same. Very, very few have survived: two in Holland and maybe a dozen all over the world.

LILAC
▧ ▧ THE THIRD JAPANESE ▧ ▧

Very shortly after the Yamaha YD 2, and still in 1961, we meet the Lilac LS 18. Again, in Holland. This was the model Masashi Ito designed in 1959, and was to be built in his new factory. In 1961 the twice-financed factory started to build a range of vee-twin ohv four-strokes, ranging in capacity from 125 to 350cc. The 250cc LS 18 was the main model, a

(left) **The other makers tried to create something like the Super Cub. This is the two-stroke Yamaha MF 30 (50cc), which had some success, but never on the scale of the Honda.**

(right) **Four-speed unit of the later version of the C 110.**

(top left) **Lilac sales brochure of 1960**: the layout is far more modern than that of Honda brochures of the time. The models range from 125 to 300 cc.

(top right) **Lilac C 81** of 125cc, 1960. Shaft drive and a twin-cylinder engine for a 125.

LS 18 of 250cc (1961) was the best-known Lilac. Unfortunately, teething troubles meant that it was unable to rescue the Lilac concern from financial straits.

Biggest Lilac of its time was the 300cc MF 39 Lancer. Most exports of this model were to Australia.

touring bike, like the Honda Dream. It rather resembled the Yamaha YD 2, as well. The Dream remained popular, even after the CB 72. On paper, the Lilac LS 18 promised to be a better bet. It was a relatively large machine with a telescopic front fork; and 17in wheels with wide tyres looked good. Shaft drive to the rear wheel was a classy feature, as on BMWs. The Lilac had an electric starter and winkers, like the Dream. It was a four-stroke and its engine looked really impressive. It was neatly finished: nice castings and good shapes. Eighteen horse power gave 75mph. Not bad for a 1961 touring machine. The LS 18 should have held a place between the Dream and the Hawk. Contemporary reporters were thrilled with the Lilac. The sound emitted by the mufflers was described as a 'cross between a BMW and a Harley'. In the first year, 65 were sold in Holland. Note: Holland is a small country and in the sixties between 2,000 and 4,000 motorcycles were sold per year – all makes and capacities combined.

The Lilac was found to be both sporty and comfortable. Things seemed likely to go well for the company. Then the history of the fifties overtook the Dutch importer, Nimag. It turned out that Masashi Ito's luck was over. The bikes began to break down.

There were teething troubles. Some were understandable, and some were simply stupid! If an oil passage is not properly drilled, it can be a production error: oil does not reach the big-end bearings, or at best too little oil gets there. The crank seizes (especially with Europeans used to riding at full throttle for as long as possible). Another poor detail in the Lilac's design goes back to the Victoria Bergmeister, the motorcycle from which the Lilac is derived. The piston rings are thick and heavy. Fluttering in the ring grooves in the pistons makes them wear out their seats. Then the rings break. And

V stands for vee engine. Note neat integration of winkers into the tail light; this is a 1961 LS 18.

(right) **Speedo shape recalls European style of the fifties.**

Lilac LS 18 engine, prior to rebuilding. The castings are well made; the internals are not. Piston ring grooves have widened because of fluttering of the rings. Lilac pistons often cracked from top to gudgeon pin.

if they do not break, they wear very rapidly. Ironically, Lilac pistons were made by ART, the factory that made Honda pistons. The design of parts was done by the motorcycle manufacturer; ART only has production responsibility, which helps to explain why the same factory could make good and bad

products at the same time. The gears in the shaft-drive were of poor quality, as well. They would literally melt in extreme use. Irony … in Belgium there is a butter called Lilac! The shaft-drive gears were made by Brother at their knitting machine factory. In practice, most Lilacs break down

Very few, possibly a couple of dozen, Lilac LS 18s have survived.

terminally after 9,000 miles or so. I have seen 13 among the 173 Lilacs sold in Holland, and it was more or less the same fate for all of them.

In Great Britain no Lilacs were sold; in America there were moderate sales. It took them a little longer to break down because Americans ride a little slower than Europeans (because of strict speed limits); but in a while the story was the same. Ito felt forced to ignore the problems. He faced a double financial burden. America has a reputation around the world for suing suppliers of faulty goods, and this is what happened. One claim after another cost Ito dearly. He tried his luck with another model; this time he wanted to be absolutely sure he'd got it right. No designing of his own was done; there was no time.

Since 1963 a beautiful prototype of a 150cc boxer-engined Lilac, the C 105, had been waiting in the wings. It had overhead camshafts, driven by bevel gears. A dozen or so had been built. Ito did not dare to gamble on his own design. He took a BMW R 50 engine and more or less copied it. It was not possible to copy it exactly, for BMW might sue Ito for stealing the design. Indeed, BMW had investigated the possibility of a law-suit. They found there were too many differences between the models to be successful in court. Construction details were

different in the R 92 engine. Roller bearings in the crankshaft, for example. Ito tried to avoid errors, because the BMW was a good engine. By sticking as close as possible to the original, Ito thought that the 500cc R 92 Lilac would have fewer problems. Well, it was indeed better than the LS 18; but not much better. *Motor* of Holland tested it, and was upbeat about the model, but imports never arrived. The rest of Europe, too, refused to import them. America was the market Ito concentrated on. The Lilac R 92 was sold there under the name of the company itself, namely, Marusho. It was now 1964. The model was called the Marusho 500 ST, and it was a very good-looking bike, far better looking than a BMW. The cycle parts of the old LS 18 had been modernised with a slim chrome front guard and 18in wheels. Again, there seemed to be a promising motorcycle on offer. And again, it was not to be. After 575 units had been built, the first modifications were made. When pushed along, the engine overheated, not as much as the LS 18 had done, but enough to cause failures. The bikes held together longer than before, only to run into meltdown problems with the secondary transmission gears.

The overheating problems were overcome, and the improved version of the 500 ST was called the 500 ST Magnum. Too late; the make's reputation was critically damaged and there were few sales. Only 183 Magnums were built. Even an electric-starter 500cc boxer, the 500 ST Electra, could not tempt customers. A pity, for now they were good: 108 were built.

Ralph Walker on his 1966 Marusho ST 500 Magnum Electra, one of only 108 built. Ralph has sorted out the history of the Marusho/Lilac factory from Mr Masashi Ito.

To show what might have been, look at this marvel! Overhead camshaft (driven by bevel and gear) flat-twin engine, shaft drive, huge brakes, slim lines... like the Honda CB 92 Benly, this 1964 Lilac 125cc C 103 is pure art. There was a 150 cc version too; six are believed to have been be built.

In 1967 the curtain falls for Marusho. The money involved in the claims can not be raised, and it's all over. In late 1967 the factory is declared bankrupt. Ito had been allowed to be part of the Japanese expansion drive; one could say that he tripped over the threshold.

Strangely, the American importer did not go broke. It still existed in 1981, albeit in 'sleeping' form. They simply sold the parts they had. In 1990 very few of the 500cc boxer Marushos survived, and most of those were in the USA, of course. There are one or two Marushos in Japan. A handful can be found in Germany and one is in Holland. The latter (guess where!) is one of the 183 Magnums, not the test bike of 1967. All the bikes outside the USA are exports from that country. Masashi Ito was running a little

hotel in the 1980s… If he had not gone bankrupt in 1959, Masashi Ito would have overcome the technical problems. He may not have been as zealous as his old teacher, Soichiro Honda, but Ito was anxious to make a good product. After all, that is what he had done throughout the fifties with his singles and side-valve boxer models. If we ignore the mechanical mishaps, the finish of the vee-twins must be acknowledged as being very good. The LS 18 in my collection is a nice example. Sold new in 1965, it broke down in 1966 after 13,576 kilometres (approximately 9,000 miles). The bike already had a reputation in '66, so it was abandoned after the owner found out what was wrong: the pistons were cracked. The bike stood under an open shelter, with the cylinders in a crate. In 1986, the camshaft was

Finally some real opposition for Honda's CB 72. The Yamaha YDS 3 of 1965 was the first Yamaha to hit the sales lists hard. The howl of the intakes will be remembered even more vividly than the exhaust note by anyone who ever owned a YDS 3.

still shiny, and the crankshaft serviceable. The corroded aluminium was very easily polished with a cloth. In fact, only the chrome had given up. It is fair to say that the vee-twin line of Lilac had everything needed to become a success; and this can't be said of the boxer models. Why buy a Lilac if a BMW is at least as good? The vee range would have started with a 125cc. The top line could be anything. How would Moto Guzzi have developed if there had been a range of Lilacs? The other makes in Japan had already accepted Lilac as a competitor. If only … We would have had to speak now of the Big Five!

YAMAHA'S SECOND CHANCE

In Japan, Yamaha's fortunes prospered (as we have mentioned in the chapter on the fifties); but the story in the rest of the world was rather different. The YD 2 was not a success in 1961. Honda was one step ahead, not only on the street, but on the racetrack. Each time Yamaha made a move, Honda appeared to be one step in front. In 1961 a YD 2 would have been a serious rival to a '59 C 71 Dream! But in 1961 Honda had the CB 72 on parade. The much improved C 72 tourer was faster than the YD 2. But Yamaha still had their old Asama racer, developed into the 1968 YDS 1 sportsbike. That one was the right design, albeit in very crude form. It was marketed outside Japan, in the USA and Australia, but only in small numbers. Still, this was the model that showed Yamaha the right way to go. It had 18in wheels and a tubular frame and a telescopic front fork. Those were the key ingredients that had made the CB 72 so successful. Yamaha made it a matter of honour to challenge the CB 72. "Anything Honda can do we can do better". The

YDS 1 was developed into the YDS 2. But it wasn't a success; at petrol stations there was no supply of two-stroke oil in those days, so you had to take the stuff with you and mix it on the spot. Very inconvenient! And performance was not good enough. Very few were sold in America and none in Europe – except for the one or two that found their way to the UK.

In 1964, the next development appears: the YDS 3. And with this one, Yamaha was in business! The cosmetics, with the attractive side covers and chrome guards, made it a handsome motorcycle. Twenty-four horsepower translated into a decent performance. It had a five-speed gearbox, one up on the Honda. Technical finesse still was not on a par with Honda (imperfect hardening of the gears caused breakdowns); but Yamaha could compensate with features Honda didn't have. Finally, there was the Autolube system which eliminated the oil-petrol mixing drama. Now one could hit the highway on the Yamaha without a care. The YDS 3 may not have been faster than the Honda, but it was certainly not slower. And its acceleration was better.

In the end, Yamaha YDS 3 was a worthy competitor for the Honda CB 72. In my view, Hondas of the era are more durable; but its five speeds, and the stylish mudguards and generally sporting character made many friends for the Yamaha. With the YDS 3,

The engine of the Yamaha YDS 3 was not hyper advanced. It still had the clutch on the crankshaft. But at last the Adler had been surpassed, the Yamaha having far more power with its two carburettors. The centre bearings of the crank often collapsed under the stress of high revolutions. The gears of the transmission in this unit have broken. Torque on the cogs, combined with hardening errors, caused the trouble. Cylinders are made of cast iron.

It may not have been so advanced as the road-going models of the competition, but this Yamaha TD 1 C, based on the street YDS 5, was the production racer to have if you were to win. Many tuning modifications were available, together with general back up from the factory.

Yamaha sold substantial numbers of these bikes in all the important markets. But improvements were called for, as the quality of the transmission gears of the YDS 3 was low: tooth form and the hardening process left a lot to be desired. Many gearboxes gave trouble. The problems seemed almost as bad as Lilac had experienced. (But Yamaha handled the warranty aspect far better than Lilac.) The oil pump that controlled mixing of the fuel and oil was driven through the gearbox. If you were waiting for the traffic lights to go green, first gear engaged and clutch in operation, the pump was not driven, so a full-throttle take off on green would be done on oil-free fuel. Piston seizure was not uncommon. As with Honda, development of the model continued, even during production. The taillight was enlarged, the shape of the front fender modernised, and a two-tone seat introduced. Yamaha brought in two-tone metallic colours to contrast with the chrome fenders at a time when Honda relied on straight colours, to combine with grey mudguards. The Yamaha won this contest, looking a little more modern than the Honda. Then Yamaha brought out a 305cc version of their two-fifty, the YM 1. Instead of merely boring out the cylinders, Yamaha also changed the stroke. Performance, it has to be said, was hardly better than that of the YDS 3; but torque at low engine speeds was slightly improved. The first round in the 305 class went to the Honda Super Hawk ....

In the USA the two companies competed in the scramblers' market: Honda CL 72 and CL 77 versus Yamaha YDS 3 C and YM 1 C. Honda again was the winner, with its all-new tubular frame for the CL. Scramblers do not sell well in Europe, for there are no vast deserts where one can go off road. When a European goes off road, it is in competition, on a laid-out circuit, and then a competition motocross machine is the chosen tool.

Summing up the Japanese motorcycle markets outside Japan as they existed in 1965, we can see that they had established a place, conclusively. The small-capacity classes were dominated by the Japanese factories: Honda with the CB 72 and the CB 77, Yamaha with the YDS 3 and a few YM 1s. Then Honda C 92 and CB 92. Honda C 100 Super Cubs, and a few C 110s were leading bikes in the 50cc class.

Honda is moving up in capacity; and we meet a 'new' make, Suzuki. The Suzuki T 20 and Honda's Black Bomber make clear that, again, technical standards are rising. Model ranges grow. Honda brings out a superb 90cc lightweight, the S 90. Suzuki comes up with the A 100 single with rotary disc induction. Yamaha announces the YL 1 Twinjet, a 100cc twin-cylinder two-stroke. Like the old CB 92 from Honda, this is a real thoroughbred. The Benly Super Sports has a successor, the CB 125 SS, that looks like a shrunken CB 72.

In Holland sales of motorcycles as a whole reach the absolute nadir of just 2,000 units but within that total the Japanese see their sales go up. They really flourish from now on: 50% of the bikes sold in the Netherlands are Japanese in 1966. Other European countries are all set to follow Holland's example.

SUZUKI T 20
■ WHEN TWO ARE FIGHTING... ■

Honda and Yamaha were battling each other fiercely in 1966, most strongly in the 250cc class. The two-fifties of the mid-60s can be compared to the 600s of today. Honda's CB 72 and Yamaha's YDS 3 were the big rivals. And then, seemingly out of the blue, came the Suzuki T 20. Shunzo Suzuki's company was enjoying a great comeback. In Britain a few machines were sold in 1965, but it was 1966 when the T 20 really hit all-important world markets in significant numbers. The failure of the T 10 in 1963 was soon forgotten; that one had been last of the line of Colledas that started with the Colleda TT of 1956.

Then came the Twin Ace, then the TB, finally a few TCs. The TBs were developed into the T 10. It was not revolutionary enough to make an impact. But the T 20, also known as the Super Six, or X 6 in the States, was a major step forward. The name of the bike refers to the six-speed gearbox – absolutely new for a standard streetbike.

Now, at a stroke, both the Honda CB 72 and the Yamaha YDS 3 had become old-fashioned! A T 20 outruns them easily. It looks more modern as well. The T 20 is, in fact, so modern that 20 years later the construction principles of two-strokes still haven't changed. The crankcase split horizontally. The three main bearings are clamped between the halves. Primary drive is by helical gears. The clutch sits on the mainshaft of the transmission. Cylinders are no longer of cast iron; the T 20's are in light-alloy, with iron liners. They weight far less and the cooling capacity is greater and they can still be bored and honed. Piston-port induction is employed. The quality of finish is superb, and there's plenty of power on tap, 29 horsepower to shift 135kg. No wonder the bike is fast, and not only by two-fifty standards. The brochure speaks of a "100 miles per hour motorcycle". And in practice it almost reached that speed.

Yamaha was first, but now Suzuki too has an automatic mixing system for oil and petrol and it is even more advanced than Yamaha's. The oil is not just forced into the intake manifolds, but plastic

Suzuki arrives! The 1966 T 20 Super Six (or X 6) did what the Dream had done for Honda: it put Suzuki on the map. No Adler roots in this all-new model, which went on to beat the CB 72.

I bought this 1966 machine in 1974 and never restored it. Today it can still outperform many brand-new 250s, which indicates how far ahead of its contemporaries it was. Add watercooling and modern styling and you'd be ready to take on any 1990s 250...

leads also bring the oil into the main bearings. As a consequence, less oil is required; delivery of the pump is controlled by engine rpm in combination with throttle position. The latter controls the stroke of the plunger in the pump. The YDS 3 error in the drive-train of the oil pump has been avoided by Suzuki. Having first gear engaged and the clutch pulled in does not prevent the pump from doing its job.

Speedometer and tachometer are integrated in one instrument, as in so many Japanese bikes of the sixties. We will even see this feature back in the Katana range of the 80s. Detail finish is very neat, even better than on Honda and Yamaha. Even the handlebar rubbers display an 'S' logo. The brakes of all Japanese 250s are miles ahead of the competition. Up front on the T 20 we find an 205mm duplex

drum, at the rear a 180mm. Handling is as good as the braking. This, combined with the speed of the bike, makes it unsurprising that many T 20s finish at the front of long-distance races, especially in the UK. After a winning Triumph Bonneville in the 650 class often a Suzuki would be second; before all the other 650s. The only preparation usually required

was fitting a bigger fuel-tank.
In Germany Ernst Leverkus from *Das Motorrad* could not wait for the Suzuki to be imported into his country. He went to Holland and rode the first 'German' T 20 around the Nürburgring.
The exhaust of a T 20 makes one of the nicest twin two-stroke sounds around. There's hardly any

The earlier Colledas and the T 10 have nothing in common with this Suzuki T 20. The T 20 was more advanced than any contemporary European design.

Compact six-speed unit of the Suzuki T 20: construction details, such as the horizontal split of the crankcases, are up to date even now.

mechanical noise; only the exhaust is heard. But on full song, the engine vibrates quite violently; the engine bolts of the first series broke frequently as a result. And the front fork has hardly any damping capacity. The shock absorbers are nice to look at, but performed poorly. British forks and shocks are better. If you want to keep the T 20 'awake', you have to maintain the integrated rev-counter needle at over 5,500rpm. If you do this, the T 20 really flies. Yet it is possible to cruise at no more than 3,000rpm all day. Plugs will not foul. Gears snick in nicely. A peculiar feature of the six-speed gearbox is the guard against direct down shifting from second to first. You automatically end up in neutral when downshifting and changing up can be done while skipping neutral. Many later motorcycles of the eighties were to have this feature.

One of the few blemishes in the T 20's otherwise impressive packaging is the mid-range carburation. With the engine at between 4,500 and 5,500rpm, the carburation is seemingly totally confused; it's as if the choke has been left in operation. Once past 5,500rpm, the racer inside the T 20 comes out. Riding hard is a joy, and handling is very positive, despite the poor suspension. Fuel consumption is low, and lighting at the level of candle power (but it always works).

Yes, the T 20 was a hit. It was both reliable and fast. It was a street racer capable of carrying a commuter on his daily trips. Suzuki was on the map. In 1968 the T 20 was the most popular 250 in Holland, despite having been only two years on the market. The T 20 was sold from 1966 to 1969 and in this period nothing important was changed. The gusseting of the frame around the headstock became heavier in 1968, making handling even better. The T 20 was followed by the T 250, in 1970, when the crank was carried by four bearings. Gearbox and clutch became heavier. But, broadly, the bike remained virtually the same as its predecessor. Weight went up a little, and it's true that the styling took on a more modern aspect.

T 20 features: combined engine/road speed instruments, powerful duplex front brake, six-speed engine-gear unit. There were no other six-speed standard motorcycles on the market at the time.

KAWASAKI

Just as Suzuki was really making an impact, Kawasaki Motorcycles met the press, and the A 1 Samurai was announced. Before we come to that, however, we must go back a little. We have seen how Yamaha and Suzuki failed at their first attempt, and now Kawasaki had much the same experience – only they reacted so fast that, in hindsight, it looks as if they had anticipated problems. This is the background...

In 1963, the Meihatsu and Meguro factories, both owned by the Kawasaki Heavy Industries group, joined forces to produce motorcycles under the Kawasaki banner. At first, the bikes were re-badged Meihatsu and Meguro. The 250 SG was a Meihatsu and the W 1 a revamped Meguro K 1 Stamina. The 250 was not able to compete effectively against a Honda CB 72 or a Yamaha YDS 3. The W 1,

however, was considered to be exactly what the motorcycling public wanted. The American market was there to be conquered. As we have seen, in the 1950s the big Meguro was quite an improvement over the original BSA design as far as 'technology' was concerned. Even more than the old Meguro, the Kawasaki closely followed the looks of the BSA A 10. In 1965, no big bikes had been exported from Japan, and so it was expected that the W 1 would be a success in America. Kawasaki figured that performance would be a match for the competition; and, accordingly, much was expected of the 650cc W 1. How wrong they were! Nobody in the USA had heard of Kawasaki motorcycles. Small bikes from Japan? OK; but big guns? That was another matter entirely. The punters said: Why should we buy something that looks like a BSA, but isn't a BSA? Americans would rather buy a Spitfire, if they wanted a fast big twin. The Spitfire from BSA looked

Kawasaki W1 of 1967 was a re-badged Meguro. Very few reached Europe. In the States, Kawasaki expected success with this model. But given choice, Americans preferred BSA's Spitfire, disregarding the better quality of the W1.

far more modern than an A 10, which of course was the pattern for the W 1. On top of that, the Kawasaki was more expensive than a Spitfire. The fact that a W 1 was technically superior to the BSA did not appear to cut much ice, for Americans were not convinced that it was superior. It did, however, have a better finish than the BSA.

Another important point was that Americans in the sixties put much store by 0-50 mph times, and in this department the BSA was a decisive winner. In Europe Kawasaki suffered much the same experience, with the result that very few W 1s were sold; even Holland, try-out market supreme, only imported 11 W 1s.

Australia, however, was a country where the people did accept the W 1. It became – almost – popular. Unfortunately, Australia was not a very important market. In Japan itself the story was very different because, for one thing, police forces were keen to buy Kawasakis. In 1968 a W 2 with two carburettors was introduced; in 1972 a W 3. But by that date it really was something of a dinosaur. The matter of gearbox design is worth mentioning. A W 3 had seven links in the pedal action. Why? Because changing legislation meant that all motorcycles had to place gear shift control on the left side of the bike; and of course operation on the W 1 had been on the right. W 3 models had a double disc brake at the front, and shared its taillight design with the 750 triple H 2 that was in production. Engine covers were modernised, with big 'W' and 'Kawasaki' logos cast in. But basically, technically, nothing had changed. In 1974 the last W 3 came off the assembly line. The Japanese police still ran W 3s while a powerbike such as the Z 1 (900) was available. After the W series came the twin-cylinder Z 750 which exhibited more technical fripperies but was in fact in many ways inferior to the W models. The successor to the W also has virtues. I can mention that riding a Z 750 is very agreeable. The comfort of the machine and the tractability at low revs make it a nice tourer. Trouble with this model is that it looks too much like a Z 1, and does not perform like one; it is a *touring* bike.

KAWASAKI'S SECOND ATTACK ON THE MARKET

Soon after the launch of the W 1 it became clear to Kawasaki's top brass that success wouldn't come easily, and so they evolved a clear-cut marketing strategy. As with Honda and Yamaha (as well as Suzuki, by the way) before them, Kawasaki decided that the 250cc class was to be tackled first. By 1967, however, there were three very strong contenders in the 250 market: the CB 72, the YDS 3 and the T 20. Appropriating a share of the market against such strong opposition would be a monumental task. Kawasaki decided to make a 'fresh sheet of paper' start. The public's requirements, they were sure, were speed, and speed, and speed! A two-stroke? OK, but no messing with mixing oil and gasoline. What people wanted was a road-going racer. And that is exactly what they got. The Kawasaki A 1 Samurai, announced in 1966, marketed in 67, proved a hit. Just like Suzuki with the T 20, Kawasaki had it right this time. Now they were in business.

The Samurai had a stainless-steel front mudguard, and a chromed guard at the rear. The fuel tank was painted in flashy metallic red and white, or metallic blue and white; no chrome tank panels this time. There was a double cradle frame with a chromed front fork with rubber gaiters. The traditional combination of rev-counter and speedometer in the headlight housing was used. There were powerful drum brakes, a duplex up front and a single unit at

Kawasaki caused historians some confusion over model names. There have been W 1, W 2 and W 3 models. For each model, there were several variations, sometimes overlapping. The firm kept no records. All engine and frame numbers include 'W 1'. Sales brochures like this one are not a reliable source...

the rear. The engine was a marvel, all aluminium, with five-speed transmission. The alloy cylinders were fed by two carburettors on each side of the crankcase and induction was by rotary disc, which meant that the dynamo and ignition was moved behind the cylinders, driven by three helical gears. A pump took care of injecting the proper amount of oil into the intake manifolds left and right of the engine. This really was no less than a Grand Prix racing engine detuned for the streets!

The Yamaha YDS 3 was easily outclassed by the Kawasaki newcomer, as was the now ageing Honda CB 72. After the struggle between Honda and Yamaha for the lead in the 250 class, the fight was now between Suzuki's T 20 and the new A 1 Samurai.

The T 20 had simple piston-port induction, but this was compensated for by other features, such as the six-speed gearbox and a more refined oil system – as well as the proven reliability of the Suzuki.

On the road, in practical terms, it was usually the Suzuki that emerged as winner. The trouble with the Kawasaki was that it was more sensitive to sloppy preparation or even bad weather! The indirect drive for the ignition was another factor, inviting inaccurate timing. Still, clubman races became more and more interesting as Kawasakis came to the line. Tuned CB 72s were still formidable and the Yamaha concern had plenty of experience in tuning for racing, their TD production racers being clearly related to the YDS. There were now four makes of competitive motorcycles in clubman racing, each with its advantages and flaws.

A few months later, but still in 1967, Kawasaki took the next step, by bringing out a 350. The A 7 Avenger was a more refined, enlarged version of the Samurai with an oiling system as sophisticated as that of the Suzuki – which meant that using mixed fuel could lead to trouble. The main bearings relied on directly injected oil, which would not reach the bearings if it was diluted with the fuel.

The Avenger's cylinders had larger fins, technically for better cooling, but adding usefully to the 'big-bike' looks of the 350. Apart from bigger tyres, the cycle parts were as for the Samurai. Cosmetically, the 350 Kawasaki amounted to a step back, in my opinion, with chrome panels on the fuel tank. However by the standards of the day it cannot be

The second chance for Kawasaki was this superb 250cc A 1 Samurai. It became for Kawasaki what the CB 72, the YDS 3 and the T 20 were for Honda, Yamaha and Suzuki.

Sales brochure from 1968 shows that after 1968 the 250 and 350 models from Kawasaki shared the same styling (unlike the 1967 versions).

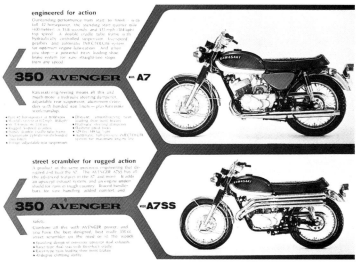

model A7 <INJECTOLUBE>

This is the first 350 from Kawasaki, the A 7 Avenger. It arrived on the market months after the 250 Samurai, representing hi-tech in a more or less conservatively styled machine.

denied that the Avenger was a good looker. It is just that styling did not match technical development. This 350 really performed well. On a good day, top speed could be 105mph. I recall a (recent) battle between a 1967 Avenger and a 1984 Yamaha RD 350

YVPS. All right, the classic had been well restored and the Yamaha was in everyday condition after years on the streets; but the Kawasaki was quicker! What impressed me most was that the handling of the old bike was in no way inferior to that of the Yamaha. Suspension and braking showed the difference in age; but in fact the Kawasaki's shortcomings could have been easily overcome. These were, in short, worthy competitors and the match served to show how advanced the Kawasaki 350 Avenger was. (Unfortunately, the flaws of the Samurai were also those of the Avenger: the indirect ignition drive, now with two gears, and sensitivity to weather conditions resulted in many seizures.)

The 250cc A 1 Samurai and the 350cc A 7 Avenger shared a common styling after 1968. The chrome on the Avenger disappeared, in favour of Samurai-pattern paintwork. Only the cylinder fins and the tyres were notably different. In 1968 the Meguro-inspired old fuel tank emblem disappeared, making way for a large, painted 'Kawasaki' logo; 1969 was the last year of the teardrop-shaped tank, and the combination mph/revs dial was traded in for

The 1968 A 1 and A 7. These models put Kawasaki on the map.

Bridgestone was too late with this mechanical marvel, the 175 Dual Twin. For the US there was the hi-pipe Hurricane Scrambler, advanced and well made. Bridgestone was a threat to the other makers and was forced to withdraw.

separate clocks. Port timing became more radical, for greater performance. This was to counter Honda's speed advantage with their 750. In 1971 the A 1 and A 7 twins were replaced by the S 1 and S 2 piston-port triples of 250 and 350cc.

BRIDGESTONE

We have seen that 1966 and 1967 were notable years in the history of the Japanese motorcycle. The Bridgestone Tyre Company, no less than the other makers, felt that the time was right for a big breakthrough. Mr Shojiro Ishibashi started making tyres in the city of Kurume in 1935. Pre-war, it was fashionable in Japan to use an English-sounding name. Ishibashi means something like 'stone to build a bridge from' – so he called his tyres Bridgestones. In the late fifties a small part of the factory was involved in motorcycles because the directors of the company considered bikes to be a useful sort of hobby. The motorcycles didn't bring

in any money, but their costs were low. Mediocre Bridgestones of 50, 60 and 90cc could survive the hard times of the late fifties under the umbrella of the parent company – more or less like Meguro and Meihatsu, under Kawasaki. In the same fashion, Bridgestone had taken over the engine department of the Fuji factory in 1960.

Let's move on a few years, to 1964. Pointer and Tohatsu are two of the makers that close down in that year; Tohatsu had nice twin-cylinder racers of 50 and 125cc. These bikes were ready for racing. Kazuo 'Johnny' Honda (remember no relative to Soichiro) had taken Tohatsus to Europe where some had appeared in circuit racing. The development engineers for the Tohatsu racers came over to Bridgestone, bringing works drawings as well as a complete machine. The result of this injection of expertise was that in 1965 Bridgestone developed the 175 Dual Twin. Sales began in 1966. Where the Tohatsu racer had piston-port induction, the new Bridgestone was equipped with rotary discs, after the style of the Kawasakis that were being developed at that time. Anxious not to go into direct competition with the other Japanese companies, Bridgestone chose a capacity which had been neglected in the sixties: the 175cc class used to be important in the Europe of the fifties, but by 1965 had become extinct. No other Japanese maker produced a bike in this category. The models that Bridgestone exported were the 90cc single and the new 175. They went to Britain and Holland; the 90 was reasonably successful in the UK, but not in Holland. The 175 Dual Twin and the scrambler version, the Hurricane Scrambler, by contrast, were liked everywhere, including the USA. Technically speaking, the 175 was a real beauty. You could call it a Kawasaki engine with Suzuki-like quality. The finish of the castings was impeccable; alloy cylinders with chrome-plated bores were well manufactured. There were no cooling problems.

Using the lever on the engine one could choose between 'four-speed, rotation shift' and 'five-speed, return shift'. The first option was popular in Japan, the second in the West.

Power was registered at 20bp, from 177cc; not a bad figure at all. The bike would top 70mph. Perhaps importantly, the styling was not really revolutionary. One could mistake a 175 BS for a Suzuki T 200 (a better known 1967 model of 200cc) or a T 20. The gearbox had an unusual feature stemming from a little handle on the crankcase which, in one position, gave the rider the usual five-speed gearbox; in the other position, there was, in effect, a four-speed gearbox, with repeating operation. After fourth, which was top gear, you could shift directly to neutral; and first; and so on. It used to be a popular arrangement in Japan and was featured on the very first Honda Dreams that reached Europe. Honda abandoned the idea in 1960; now it was back, on the 1966 Bridgestone 175. Obviously, for Westerners, the four-speed option was completely obsolete.

The Bridgestones were really very good. Until 1975 they were ahead of the field in 125 class racing in Europe. Since there were no spares, this must rank as a tribute to the reliability and the high level of engineering achieved.

Encouraged, the company produced the 350 GTR, along the lines of the 175 Dual Twin. Now they would meet the competition head on in the completely new 350cc class. (New for the Japanese, that is.) The 1967 Bridgestone 350 GTR was, indeed, as good as the 175. It was neatly styled, with an impeccable finish. There were two mounting positions for the rear shocks. The engine was built on the lines of the 175. There were similarities with a Kawasaki Avenger unit. There also were differences, of course, like the dry clutch on the BS. If parked next to a Suzuki or a Kawasaki, the Bridgestone GTR dwarfed them. This was one successful motorcycle, and if it had been 1956 when it appeared, not 1967, who knows what Bridgestone motorcycles might have achieved.

But in the sixties, it was not to be; the competition took measures. Bridgestone would not be allowed to take Lilac's place. The firm was given a clear choice: either to be a major tyre producer, with the Big Four as customers, or meet the assembled competition head on in a battle Bridgestone could not hope to win, or even, possibly, survive. It was 1970 when the production of motorcycles was ordered to be stopped. Other sources speak of 1972. This is not likely. The catalogues stop mentioning the Bridgestones after 1970; 8,000 Bridgestone 350 GTRs had been made by that time. Few survive. There is a handful of them in Britain, one in Holland;

The Yamaha YDS 5 displayed many improvements over the YDS 3 (note: no 'YDS 4' existed). Finally the clutch had been moved to the mainshaft. This 1967 model was the first really sophisticated Yamaha.

This was the model that closed the door for Bridgestone. The 350 GTR was too big a threat for the other makers. It was a powerful, advanced model with six speeds, dry racing clutch and disc-valve induction.

nobody knows how many there are in the US. The little singles were to survive into the 1970s. The rights of production of the 100cc single was sold to the small Hodaka firm. Hodaka made a scrambler with Bridgestone technology and sold it to the USA. No noticeable development took place in Hodaka, and it has to be said that a Hodaka Wombat is only a poorly made copy of the Bridgestone. The catalogues mention 250cc Hodaka motocross machines up to 1982, but nobody ever saw one.

Yamaha's answer

As we have seen, 1967 was a busy year, with many new models coming on to the market. During the preceding years there had been the battle between Honda and Yamaha – primarily between the CB 72 and the YDS 3. Suzuki and Kawasaki had made their debut in the so important 250 cc class. The YDS 3 needed improvement if Yamaha wanted to stay in the race. The successor was not called the YDS 4; Japanese superstition has it that '4' is an unfortunate number; like '13' in our culture. So the new Yamaha sportsbike was called YDS 5. It is very clear that it was designed to take on and defeat Honda's CB 72. The new Yamaha had a 'dynastart' – a dynamo that can operate as a starter motor. Yamaha had gone in

for this feature only because the Honda had it; after all, a two-stroke was very easy to start on the kickstart. In fact, on the Yamaha, the dynastart wasn't a success, because the weight of the rotor caused crankshaft problems. But in other respects

Modern styling and old techniques on view in the 1968 Yamaha DS 6, a typical "in-between" model. It successor was to strike out from the technical path followed by the old models.

the YDS 5 was superb. The primitive switches of the YDS 3 were replaced by die-cast items; the old YDS 3 oil pump problem was solved by having it driven directly by the crankshaft; the heavy iron cylinders of the YDS 3 made way for all-alloy cylinders. The liners were still iron, however, so wear could be overcome by boring out for oversize pistons. The hardening process of gearbox parts had been mastered and gear selection was quicker and more certain. The sensitive crankshaft-mounted clutch of the 3 series was replaced by a better designed item on the mainshaft of the YDS 5.

One of the main features that put Yamaha at a disadvantage had been retained, however. The vertical split of the crankcases – just like the Adler of 1956 – was still present, and of course seemed out of date in comparison with Suzuki or Kawasaki. But Yamaha's goal had been simply to beat the Honda CB 72 with a luxury sportsbike. And in 1967, seven years after the Hawk, this was finally achieved. The Yamaha could beat Honda, at last. It was unfortunate that the T 20 and the A 1 had arrived on the scene! Yamaha came a poor third compared to these two. Performance was not a problem; the YDS 5 was as fast as the competition; it was 'technology' that put Suzuki and Kawasaki ahead of the Yamaha.

Racing

On the track a different story unfolded. Old-fashioned as their bikes were, Yamaha had a lot of experience in racing. A YDS 5 fitted with a dynamo from a YDS 3 was an effective racer. Yamaha riders engineered a booster port with the result that performance and cooling of the pistons were improved; it was a modification that found its way on to the production machines as well. Late in 1967, the YDS 5 was renamed YDS 5 E to take account of the new porting arrangement. The TD 1 C production racer was directly developed from the YDS 5 and became THE production racer to have.

The vast experience and the good back-up of the factory made the old-fashioned TD 1 C – 200 were built – a winner over the T 20-based TR 250, and the A 1 R as well.

THE YAMAHA DS 6

By 1968, Yamaha knew that the YDS was running out of time; the previous year had shown them the way they should be going, in the shape of the 350cc R 1. We will come to that one later. Yamaha realised that the styling of the YDS 5 was old-fashioned and that drastic measures were needed to keep up with the other makers. The successor to the YDS 5 was launched in 1968; the Y vanished in the name of the model, so it is the DS 6 that appears. The technical details were refined. The odd dynastart has gone. Square fins grace the cylinders. The tuning is now much milder, giving the DS 6 more low-end power.

(left) The 1967 Yamaha YL 1 TwinJet of 100cc was a twin-cylinder model that was almost as out of the ordinary as the Honda CB 92 and the Lilac C 103.

(right) Built on the basis of the 250 cc YDS 5 were the 305cc YM 2 as well as Scrambler models of both capacities.

Now it was the competition that looked old-fashioned. The very elegant DS 6 showed the way to the future. The nicely shaped teardrop tank retained knee rubbers but there were no chrome panels. 'Style' resulted in a smaller-capacity tank, it has to be said: form going before function. The side covers were styled to integrate with the tank. The short, chromed front mudguard and the separate speed and rpm meters were a departure from sixties convention. Strangely, the exhausts of the long-gone YD 2 returned on the DS 6.

The DS 6 was a study in styling. It made the Samurai and the Super Six outdated and even the successor to Honda's famous Hawk, the CB 250, looked bland when parked next to a DS. By the end of 1969, the DS 6 was making way for the DS 7.

HONDA CB 450
■ THE FIRST BIG JAPANESE BIKE ■

The CB 72 was showing its age late in 1965. The pure quality of the model had kept it in the sales charts, yet it was clear that a successor was called for. It was to be 1968 before Honda reacted to the flood of new models from the other makers. The British had not yet woken to the threat coming from the Hawk models. They focused on the market for motorcycles with a capacity over 500cc. In that area, no Japanese had appeared yet, apart from the few Kawasaki W 1s.

Then in 1965 a new Honda model appeared, to be marketed the following year. The 450cc CB 450 represented a technical revolution.

Japan moved one step further on with the 1965 Honda CB 450 Black Bomber, giving Triumph and Norton some real competition. This model was so advanced (don't be misled by the rather conservative styling) that it was at first not believed to be a production model.

The engine had features that previously had only been seen in exotic racing bikes. Horex, NSU, Gilera, MV Agusta and Honda factory racers had double-overhead camshafts. All these bikes were exclusively built machines for use in the grands prix. There was not, at that time, a single streetbike that the general public could buy that had these features. But the CB 450 Black Bomber had them. Even the valve springs were revolutionary: they were torsion bars instead of the usual coil springs. The 444cc engine was allowed to turn at 9,500rpm, at least 2,000rpm more than contemporary British competition managed. And if you ran the engine at that speed it would not break down. The CB 450's constant-vacuum carburettors became the pattern for what was later found on

Ignore the chrome and you see the shape of the fuel tank of a Norton Manx. The Bomber was almost as fast as a Manx...

By 1965 the combination instrument display had become commonplace. Carburettors were the first constant vacuum types to be seen. Years later, this type of carburettor is still in use, virtually unchanged.

many bikes of the seventies and even the eighties. The throttle operated only the butterfly valves; the carburettor regulated the mixture itself. It was no surprise that in spite of giving away 200cc, the CB 450 was a real competitor to the big twins from Britain. In fact, the British reacted in panic, banning the big Honda from races for standard streetbikes. Their reasoning was on the lines: "A bike with so much racing technology can not be a production model:" Quite pathetic!

As might be expected, the finish of the Bomber was outstanding. There was a rev-counter/speedometer in the headlight housing. Winkers could be ordered as extras. The front brake was a duplex unit, like that fitted to the CB 72. The electrical side included a starter motor. Honda electrics always worked – something that could not be said about the equipment on competing big bikes. The crankcase had the modern horizontal split.

There were no teething troubles; the new Honda was fast and reliable. The transmission had only four speeds, which in one respect wasn't a drawback, because no competing bike had more; but Honda was expected to give a lead, and in any case the character of the engine demanded a five-speeder. The step between first and second was big. Shifting was very accurate.

However, there was one aspect of the motorcycle that the Japanese had not mastered yet: the shock absorbers on their bikes were very poor. When Mike Hailwood first tested a Honda racer, he asked the mechanics to remove the shocks, and then threw them in a nearby pond! He was right to do so; shocks coming from Japan would really only improve by the late 70s. They were severely under-damped in 1966. Many riders of Japanese motorcycles replaced the home-produced units with Konis or Girlings. Having said that, even with the original shocks, the handling of the 450 was pretty good. Many a footrest was worn through by fast riders.

A rider felt secure on a Black Bomber; so he would go fast. To avoid upsetting the notoriously conventional Western public too much, the styling of the CB 450 was not particularly revolutionary. There was a strong semi double-cradle frame and the shape of the fuel tank had something about it of the classic Norton Manx. And the silver mudguards were valanced in the British style. It was all in the name of 'European' looks. The Dream, the Benly and the Hawk machines were much more 'Japanese' in their styling.

■ ■ Riding the Black Bomber ■ ■

One press of the button is enough. The engine ticks over. Only a few seconds after the start, the choke must be turned off. The agreeably sharp sound of the exhausts can now be enjoyed for a minute or two while the oil reaches the left side of the exhaust cam, farthest away from the plunger oil pump. You can actually hear the oil reach this point. Observe this prescription, and the 450 will do the ton repeatedly without suffering wear.

Once warmed up, the bike can be ridden hard. All day long, if you wish. Rev it up to 10,000rpm – no problem! At high rpm the engine vibrates, slightly. The carburettors help the engine pick up smoothly. This Honda is not meant as an out and out sportsbike, but can be treated as such. Only long, fast corners induce a slight weave. It will never be as bad as a contemporary BMW, however! The lights are poor. You can be seen in traffic; but you wouldn't be able to see …

Successful as the Bomber was, there were some things that prevented this Honda from being the world-beater it was supposed to be. And it was Honda that used that word, world-beater, in leaflets that went out with the CB 450. It may be true that its performance was comparable to that of a Triumph Bonnie or a BSA Spitfire; but the Bomber didn't beat the big Brits. Its weight, 180kg, had something to do with that, and another setback was the (small) size of the machine – smaller than a Triumph, a BSA or a BMW. Finally, in spite of the beautiful, technically advanced carburettors fitted to the Honda, it didn't have as much slogging, low-end power as the European top models. People were not yet used to exploiting the high revs of the Honda.

■ ■ Development ■ ■

The CB 450 underwent development in much the same way as earlier Honda models; but there was a difference. Quality did not really improve. What happened was that the customer's wishes were fulfilled. In February 1968 the CB 450 K 1 was born. The tank still had chrome panels, only now the shape of the fuel tank had been 'normalised'. And, importantly, the bike got its five-speed gearbox. Mudguards were chromed. Wheelbase was stretched a little, making the model bigger, and improving the handling. Rubber gaiters on the front forks modernised front-end looks, and the speed dials were removed from the headlamp shell, and separated. The plunger of the oil pump grew from 16 to 19 millimetres, with the benefit that oil

Double overhead camshafts were driven by chain, valves closed by torsion bars instead of coil springs.

reached the camshafts rather more quickly. Higher-compression pistons, in combination with slightly larger valves, meant an extra 2hp output. In practice, this power boost was unnoticeable, and in general the changes to the engine were not real improvements. CB 450s used in standard racing were generally four-speeders, with pistons, heads and valves of the five-speeder, because it was accepted that the four-speed engine was stronger than the more modern variant. In this guise, the 450 was competitive with the impressive Kawasaki 500 Mach 3.

As the CB 750 appeared on the market, the CB 450 lost its identity even further. The model, not being top of the line any more, with the 750 on top, now followed the lines of that famous four-cylinder, with an all-painted tank and a disc brake up front. It became something of a 'little CB 750'. The model lasted until 1974, though its glory days had in fact ended when the 1968 CB 450 K 1 appeared. The K 2, K 3, K 4 and the K 5 only differ in small details, mainly in styling. The original CB 450 was a revolution; a CB 450 K 5 was no more than a sideline. Yet I have to say that the later models are the ones that are best to ride. The engine may not be as strong as the original Bomber's, but the handling and the better-spaced gear ratios, as well as the better

Performance of a CB 450 is good enough for today. Only the front brake shows the age of this 31-year-old bike.

brakes, make a K 5 a good classic motorcycle. Warm it up gently and you have an excellent bike for daily use!

THE R 1
YAMAHA'S ANSWER
▪ ▪ TO THE BLACK BOMBER ▪ ▪

Yamaha had finally succeeded, in 1967, in catching Honda's CB 72. The YDS 5 outdid the now seven-year-old four-stroke. Unfortunately (for Yamaha), Suzuki and Kawasaki had entered the market. Any comparison of the YDS 5 with its competitors did not go favourably for the Yamaha. The old-fashioned construction of the crankcases made the engine more complex; but not better. In grand-prix racing Yamaha had had experience with several new types of engine assembly. Their GP racers, like the RD 56, had horizontally split crankcases. Now was the time to try to achieve two goals at one time: the first objective was to modernise the YDS engine; the

second, moving up in capacity. Since 1965 all two-stroke manufacturers had tried to build an engine of more than 305cc. The only manufacturer who had enjoyed some success with larger two-strokes was DKW, of Germany, the leading two-stroke manufacturer of pre-war days. The 1930s DKWs of 350 and 500cc had put out relatively little power and, even then, there had been many vibration and cooling problems. Even watercooling didn't help DKW. Creation of a big two-stroke giving decent performance was a considerable technical challenge. While Yamaha was working on what was to become the 350cc R 1, Honda had come up with the Black Bomber, and Kawasaki with their A 7 Avenger. Time was short: Yamaha would miss the boat again, if they didn't push out a new design in a hurry, so they leaked rumours to the press of a super-fast (125mph) 350cc stroker. These rumours were taken seriously, and were given a lot of coverage before the actual release of the Yamaha R 1.

The Yamaha R 1 Grand Prix was a very, very good motorcycle. It was relatively big – as big as a CB 450 – and had a huge fuel tank, like the Honda, enhanced by the big, square finning of the new alloy cylinders. Only a Bridgestone 350 GTR was larger; but of course that bike was not a threat any longer since the Bridgestone company would soon be told to stop making motorcycles. A remarkable feature of the Yamaha R 1 was its low-end power which enabled one to run it two up with just a few hundred revs showing on the rev counter, without trouble. But there was one disappointment: it would not do 125mph! The 'ton' was more than enough for the Grand Prix. And it was rather a dull looker. There were chromed panels on the big fuel tank, and a combination speed/rpm dial, as in the YDS series. The mudguards were chromed. The public did not like the looks of the R 1. (*I* love it, by the way.) It was an all-new motorcycle but the fact that it wasn't 'revolutionary' was a disappointment for many people. Having said that, we still can conclude that in the main Yamaha had succeeded in its task and that the Grand Prix was the most worthy competitor to the big Honda. It was even better than an A 7, for it was far more reliable than the Kawasaki. There were no teething troubles with the big Yamaha, and it wasn't weather sensitive, like the 350cc Kawasaki Avenger. It was thoroughly good motorcycle. The racing version, the TD 2 production racer, differed only slightly from the roadster, so there was no doubting the engine's quality. The R 1 was sold together with the YDS 5. Yamaha had found their

Yamaha, while suffering hard times in the 250cc class, enjoyed some success in the 'middle' class. The 1967 350cc R 1 was a worthy competitor for the Honda CB 450.

technical direction with the R 1. The 1968 DS 6 would show the way in styling. The R 1 was sold in the US and, in Europe, only in Holland. The R 2 was not sold in Europe at all, and it was the R 3 that started to be marketed in larger numbers. The R 2 and R 3 were developments in styling towards the DS 6 line, and when the time came to update the DS 6 and the R 3, a decision was taken to bring the

two lines together. The technical construction of the YDS series was abandoned, as was the styling of the R series. The 1970 DS 7 and the R 5 were, in fact, identical machines – the only real difference being the cylinders and pistons, to make 250 and 350cc. The mechanical outlines of the R 1 were to be continued until the 1990s. All roadgoing RDs and racing TZs were based on the R 1.

YAMAHA 350 (YR-1)

Yamaha presents its new top-of-the-line model; the big machine that brings proved Grand Prix performance to the street. It incorporates every technical and design feature developed by the Yamaha Research Institute in the last 10 years. If you're ready for a motorcycle with top acceleration, handling and maneuverability, this double-barreled 5-speed charger is the answer.

1968 SUZUKI T 500
THE ENGINE THAT COULDN'T BE MADE

For a very brief period of a few months, the Suzuki T 500 Cobra was a sensational Superbike. The announcement in 1967 had been bombastic: this was 'the engine that could not be built'. And now Suzuki proudly said they had managed to do just that. Finally, there was a full 500cc motorcycle from Japan. The Honda CB 450 and the Yamaha 350 Grand Prix represented one step forward in the Japanese conquest of the motorcycle world. Suzuki had first made a 350cc version of the T 20 which they called T 350, but in reality it could be

Cooling was very good with the wide, square fins of the R 1. Ultra-reliable engine split horizontally.

compared with a Yamaha YM 2 (305cc) or a CB 77 (also 305cc). (In this regard, we may leapfrog Kawasaki's 350 Avenger which was, physically, a small bike and was not so reliable. In any case, it would not be long before Kawasaki made their great leap forward.) Now Suzuki was ahead of them all with the T 500. In fact the statement about the engine had not been so wide of the mark, after all. All two-stroke manufacturers had tried or were trying to make a reliable, high-performance 500. The problems in making such an engine were, and are, vibration and cooling. When Suzuki claimed they had overcome the problems, expectations were high. As with the Yamaha R 1, there was a little disappointment when the first Cobra was delivered. It did not better 125mph, as had been expected. Of course, it was a beautiful machine, being well built and with detailing that was very sophisticated. Every bolt that was in sight was chrome-plated, for example. The general lines were like those of the T 20, only bigger. The fuel tank had chrome-plated panels and the valanced mudguards were even more conservatively styled than those on the 250cc T 20. It all made for a very attractive motorcycle (especially in retrospect). The fact that time was advancing rapidly was shown in the separate speedometer and rev-counter. The candy gold finish was regarded as 'bold'. The Suzuki T 500 Cobra

would reach 110mph. Later versions were a little slower, when carburettor size dropped from 34 to 32 millimetres. What was of more importance was that it could do 110 all day if you wanted. This engine was just about unburstable. And 125mph would come in sight with only light tuning of the engine, when reliability remained excellent. So now there was another competitive machine on the racetrack! Best proof of that was of course found in the person of Barry Sheene who for a season competed in grands prix on a Cobra-based TR 500 racer. On the streets the big British 650s could only beat this Suzuki on handling, because the frame of the Cobra was built just like that of the T 20. The 250 handled very well; the 500 did not. Even the duplex front brake of the Cobra was slightly undersized (Honda's Black Bomber also suffered in a similar way). There was an old construction error in the T 500: as in the old Yamaha YDS 3, the Suzuki's T 500 oil-pump is driven through the gearbox which means that if, for instance, you are sitting on a T 500 at traffic lights with first gear engaged and clutch pulled in, the oil-pump is not driven. This can be noticed because the rev-counter also gets its drive from the oil-pump; so the rev-counter falls back to zero in these circumstances. The Cobra's position at the top of the pile was not to last. October 1968 saw the end of the sensation. Two bikes were announced that would

Basically not much had changed over the years, but the GT 500 of 1976 did look rather more modern. It featured CDI ignition and, finally, a front disc brake. But it was not the top-of-the-line model that the original T 500 Cobra had been in 1968.

become the progenitors of the real modern era: the Kawasaki 500 Mach 3 and, pre-eminently, Honda's CB 750 Four. Of course, the good qualities of the Suzuki are still there, and the new bikes were not that much faster than a T 500; but the newcomers were so strikingly modern, and so exotic, that the Suzuki was somehow outdated only eight months after its sensational debut! Even the British makers had answers to the Suzuki. The Norton Commando, the BSA Rocket 3 and the Triumph Trident weren't faster, but they were far more exciting than the Cobra. It didn't mean the career of the 500 Suzuki

was over. From now on, the model was marketed as a cheap alternative to the so-called Superbikes. 'Lots of motorcycle for little money' was the name of the game now. The styling was modernised, step by step, to contemporary standards. After the 'real' Cobra there were the 1969 Cobra 2 and the 1970 Cobra 3 – the last-named with a Triumph-like rack on the fuel tank. The 1971 T 500 R model lost the rack. Then came the 1972 T 500 J, the '73 K, the T 500 L and the T 500 M. Every year, until 1975, styling changed. After 1972, the T 500 was integrated in the GT 380/550/750 triple line. Technically, nothing

The 1968 Suzuki T 500 Cobra in its original 1968 form. Styling was conventional for the time. Nowadays this version is attractive to "classic" enthusiasts.

The T 500 introduced features that were copied on many later bikes, like the vacuum-operated fuel valve. Separation of the rev-counter and speedometer marked the end of the era of combination instruments.

Tuned T 500 Cobra is
a pretty fast machine.

changed. Nor did the sales price. In 1976 the ignition became electronic and the drum front brake made way for a single disc, when the bike was renamed GT 500. There was a '76 GT 500 A and a '77 B, and there the line ended. Like a late Honda CB 450, a late T 500 is a nice bike to ride. It is only their perceived lack of charisma that keeps the later bikes from being classics. That role is reserved for the real Cobra only: the classic sixties look, then merely conservative, now makes the machine attractive. The Spanish Ossa factory was urged by its American representatives to try to make something like a T 500. Of course the existence of the Suzuki was ignored, but that is what they were trying to do. Ossa failed; they never got it right with their Yankee Twin. The technical challenge was too big. In fact, no other factory did it, and the Suzuki T 500 was to be the only modern 500cc twin two-stroke. And, yes, we know there have been a few Silk 700s, but they can not be considered production bikes, and certainly were not as 'bulletproof' as the Suzuki. So the career of the Suzuki T 500 went from Superbike, to bread-and-butter bike, to classic. It was, in fact, a unique motorcycle.

KAWASAKI H 1 500 MACH 3
▪ ▪ EXOTIC UNGUIDED MISSILE ▪ ▪

Cast your mind back, if you can, to 1968. The Beatles were growing away from each other already. Prosperity in Europe was soaring. There were student riots in Paris. It was now quite normal to change jobs, for more money, more times a year. Old-established values were under discussion. In this changing world public interest in motorcycling was growing. The motorcycle world itself was also changing rapidly.

Sales of motorcycles were creeping up, slowly. The smaller-capacity classes were in the hands of the Japanese by then, and people were getting used to that situation. Honda was the frontrunner in the 500cc class, with the CB 450 Black Bomber, and Suzuki had a good follow-up with their T 500 Cobra. The British, masters of the big machines, had their BSA Spitfire, Norton 650 SS and Atlas, and Triumph still had their famous T 120 Bonneville. These machines had established the standards for performance. And they had a charisma that the Japanese envied.

It was a fact that a well prepared Bomber or Cobra could challenge a British 650. It might even win. But the Japanese bikes were still lacking in 'character' and performance, when set against the British machines. A Japanese motorcycle to bridge that gap would need more capacity, or a technically highly developed engine. Best of all, a combination of these features. It went without saying that if a new bike was to impress it had to have top-of-the-bill maximum speed. The Kawasaki people had learned their lesson with the W 1. In order to make a name as a modern manufacturer they had brought out the Samurai and the Avenger. Now Kawasaki went one step further. They had a four-cylinder four-stroke in development. It was due to appear in 1970. Then came Honda with their announcement of a 750cc four! Kawasaki were beaten to the punch. But they

had two developments in the 500cc class that might serve, while they waited for the right time to introduce their four. There was a 500cc two-stroke twin on the lines of the 250 and 350 Kawas; and an entirely new piston-port triple of 500cc. Tests had shown that the triple was lighter, as well as faster, than the twin. So the exotic three was what Kawasaki went for.

Kawasaki's 500 Mach 3, official title H 1, made a difference to the motorcycle scene. The 'triple with the ripple' was good for stirring fierce discussion between lovers and haters. "It should be forbidden. Too dangerous," said the haters (many of them parents of young motorcyclists). "Wow, now we really have what we've always wanted, a street racer!" was the response of the people who were going to ride the H 1. However, the Kawasaki, overall, did not

Sky's the limit! The 1969 Kawasaki 500 Mach lll (official name H 1) made a splash with its sheer raw performance. One was either strongly against or very much for this projectile.

make the impact enjoyed by Honda's CB 750 – and for two reasons. One was that the capacity was 'only' 500cc. Plus, the finish and reliability of the Kawasaki were not comparable with the Honda. But still there was a great deal going for the 500. Not in a very long time had one been able to buy a three-cylinder two-stroke over the counter. And never a 125 miles per hour two-stroke!

The 60 horsepower 'Kwacker' boasted another novelty: it was the first standard motorcycle equipped with full electronic ignition. When the ignition was turned on, one heard a *beep* from under the seat, where the ignition units were placed. The fact that this first generation of a new ignition system was both very expensive and unreliable does not take away from the importance of the feature. The engine, with extensive finning on the cylinders, looked impressive under the slender red, white or anthracite-coloured fuel tank, with its characteristic ridge on the sides. There were skimpy stainless-steel mudguards. The dual-height seat and the three exhausts added to the exotic looks of the bike. A really hair-raising feature of the triple was the exhaust note. Anyone will, even today, attend to the sound of a 500 Mach 3 accelerating at full throttle. Both motorcycle enthusiasts, and bike-haters! The sound of a Kawasaki is, for two-stroke enthusiasts, what the sound of a Norton Manx is to four-stroke fans. This 500 is a love-it or hate-it machine. Everything is extreme about it. Weight is low, at 175kg. Too low, perhaps, for the handling of this rocket could be rather flighty. Unintentional wheelies can occur, for instance, during a turn... Yet the design of the frame was inspired by the world-famous Norton Featherbed. When the frame is stiffened by extra gussetting, this bike handles well. No wonder that national racing events were often won by triple riders. Even in over-the counter-trim, the bikes were capable of winning. If I am to sum up the 500 Mach 3 in one sentence, I'd say: This bike was, in effect, one great shout from Kawasaki – "Look, we are Kawasaki and we make fast motorcycles!"

■ ▨ Riding the beast ▨ ■

The engine is very peaky. There is not much power below 6,000rpm, when acceleration is mild, and plugs tend to foul. A Suzuki T 500 is far more tractable. But if you ride the Kawa as it is intended to be ridden, namely, fast, 'with intent', things change. Once past 6,000rpm all 60 horses wake up and the gallop begins. The 8,000 redline on the rev-

Model names and emblems are' becoming more prevalent than before. Compare this side cover with the one for the Honda CB 450.

(left) In its early years the H 1 had a two-leading-shoe drum brake in the front wheel that was not quite up to the job. Later disc brakes would do better.

counter is easily passed. The engine simply keeps on revving, and pulling. It does not stop at 10,000rpm. Even in comparison with modern motorcycles, performance is still quite good.

As already mentioned, the bike's handling was not up to its engine performance. The front duplex drum brake, also, was not a match for the speed of the (left) **Electronic ignition with spark divider of the H 1 was a first on a production machine. It gave trouble in radio traffic, so after a year points were back – only to be superseded by a second generation of CDI.**

Some motorcycles have the status of milestones in motorcycle history. Harley WLA, Vincent Black Shadow, Triumph Speed Twin are examples. This Honda CB 750 of 1969 merits similar respect.

bike. When approaching a sharp turn, don't forget that weak brake – or you're in for some exciting moments! On a long corner, the frame gets itself in a knot. From the perspective of a Consumer's Guide evaluation, the bike would be condemned out-of-hand. If you ask an owner/rider, you'll get a different opinion. Both views are valid.

As development of the triple proceeded, speed came down, while handling and reliability improved. Weight, too. The 1971 H 1 A still had the drum brake, but the engine was slightly detuned. Heart-shaped intakes replaced the large ports, with a bar in the centre to guide the piston rings. The engine was placed further forward in the now stiffer frame. Result: fewer wheelies! The special electronic ignition proved unreliable, so the H 1 A acquired contact-breakers. Styling moved to a more 'normal' outline. The ridge in the blue tank disappeared.

A front disc brake was specified in 1972 for the H 1 B, and colour went to bright orange. Weight was up, again, and power down. The engine reverted to electronic ignition, second generation. This was the first really effective, reliable electronic ignition system, and 15 years later would be a standard feature in the motorcycle world. The peaky, revvy character of the engine had now changed almost entirely. The 1974 version of the bike, the H 1 E, again had less power and more weight. Still, the Kawasaki remained as a fast, sporty machine, and was in fact a much better bike than the first version. There was a nice cover over the taillight, and the smoothly shaped tank now had a broad Kawasaki logo in a band, continued in the tailcover. Styling was becoming more and more 'mature'. Or staid? A 1974 Kawasaki 500 Mach 3 is a beautiful motorcycle, I think; and this was also the year in

which a much improved frame was introduced. The model was growing towards the Suzuki T 500 in character, but the Kawasaki would continue to excite people whereas the later Suzukis were relegated to the category of bread-and-butter machines.

The same we said about the H 1 E may be said about the 1975 H 1 F, in which the changes from the E were of only a minor nature. This bike, too, was a real looker. The 1976 and '77 versions, however, lost the beautiful styling and become bland. They were listed as KH 500, and had a more sophisticated lubrication system than before. The engine was set in rubber so that vibration was no longer felt by the rider. In theory, of course, a triple two-stroke should be vibration-free; the 500 Kawasaki shot some holes in this theory! Technically speaking, the KHs were the best of the series. Reliability was almost as good as that of a Suzuki T 500. To over-rev a KH was not easy, for revs would hardly exceed the redline point on the rev-counter; all very unlike the first H 1. Performance was in fact down to the level of a T 500 Suzuki. The KH 500 was very far from presenting the drop-dead impact of the original Mach 3.

If you want a real classic among these triples, go for the 1969 or 1970 model, but don't ride it too often, if you want to keep it in one piece! If you want a triple for daily use, go for the KH models. They won't let you down, ever. Nor will they excite you. In between are the 1974 and 1975 models, which are pure pieces of art to look at, from any angle. They have the air of race bikes that, somehow, have been transported to the street. These models are, if

First four-cylinder Honda CB 750 engine marked a complete turnover in motorcycle history. From now on it would be possible to buy a motorcycle over the counter offering racing performance with the reliability of an automobile. And at an affordable price.

you maintain them well, usable on a regular basis. In any case, I'd say the reader just has to ride a triple.

THE HONDA CB 750
A MILESTONE IN MOTORCYCLE HISTORY

'Modern' times begin with the CB 750. By 1969 the Japanese had evolved into being mainstream motorcycle makers. The 50, 125 and 250cc classes were almost totally Japanese. They had also established a beachhead in the middle and heavyweight classes. Bikes such as the Honda Black Bomber and the Suzuki Cobra paved the way for the next development, which was the Kawasaki 500

Four cylinders, four exhausts. The pipes were prone to rust, but they symbolised luxury in the CB 750 K 1 of 1971.

The air filter housing of the CB 750 K 1 was made of black plastic that can withstand gasoline fumes. Carburettors had desmodromic operation. On the first model the carbs opened by a one-into-four throttle cable.

Instrument housings of the CB 750 K 1 were made of metal, in contrast to the plasic used on the first series.

It is still possible to use a Honda CB 750 on a regular basis. It handles well enough, is reliable, and performs acceptably.

Mach 3, a further nail in the coffin of the British and European and American motorcycle industries. But in order to beat – conclusively – machines like the Triumph Bonneville, the Norton 650 SS, and the BSA Spitfire, a new Japanese motorcycle had to be much better than anything previously produced. The aforementioned models from Japan were good. They performed as well or better than the British bikes, but they weren't *definitively* better. And the fact that the British generally had more cc under the tank was seen as putting them almost beyond contention. Now there came along a machine from Japan that was to reshape motorcycle history. The British would not find an answer to this bike.

There had been rumours about a new 750 Honda since 1967. Everybody expected a twin. Everybody

was misled by a 'spy' photograph of a disguised CB 450 prototype. It was October 1968 when Honda showed the world what they had made. The Honda CB 750 was an ohc *four*! It had an electric starter. Five gears. Four exhausts. It had a quality of finish unseen before. Poor Norton, poor Triumph, poor BSA. The 750 Norton Commando, successor to the SS 650 and the Atlas, had only four gears and two cylinders, and ohv operation. There wasn't a starter motor. The Triumph Trident had three cylinders with ohv, no starter, and a four-speed gearbox. BSA had the Rocket Three, a similar bike to the Trident. The British bikes were nice machines, but... The Honda CB 750 was the standard they would have to meet henceforth. And they couldn't. Of course, the British factories fought back. Their racing

Plastic meters on the first CB 750 were prone to cracking.

The CB 750's engine was not to change in almost a decade. It was 'right' first time out.

Sales brochure was not modest. In 1970, this was the ultimate machine...

departments, with virtually no budget, even managed to keep up with Honda on the long-distance racing scene for a while, which was more a tribute to the mechanics and the riders than the machines. BSA ground to a halt in 1971, Norton in 1976, and Triumph had a long and moving history dragging itself from one management crisis to another until, in 1983, it was over for that concern, too.

German BMW did better than the British. They brought out the R 75/5 in an all or nothing effort, when it amounted to a decision whether to renew, or stop, producing motorcycles completely. The R 75/5 was good enough to find buyers, and signalled the start of a bright future for BMW. Even the Italian makers managed to take a slice of the market for heavy bikes. Laverda sold the GT and S models quite successfully, as did Moto Guzzi with the V 7 models. But it was the big Honda that led the market. Totally.

Honda had withdrawn from racing in 1967, after winning almost everything there was to win. The company turned to their production models, which were to perform like racers, but be as reliable as an automobile. The CB 750 was the most potent expression of this new philosophy. This one was to be an affordable Superbike (the word was invented for the CB 750, and this model alone).

Of course, four cylinders were not new in motorcycling. There had been the Ariel Square Four, the Indian Four and the Matchless Silver Hawk, all outstanding motorcycles in their own time. Now

Honda had a four-cylinder model that was so ahead of its time that it opened up a new era. Honda could not be sure that the public would accept the four. The CB 750, after all, was a complete departure from established paths in the 60s. But the 750 was the right bike at the right time! Kawasaki was outraged, and flabbergasted. They, too, had been working on a 750cc four-cylinder since the misfortune of their W 1. The Kawasaki four was due to appear in 1970. There was nothing the Kawasaki people could do other than adopt a typically British feature, the stiff upper lip, and say politely. "This is an opportunity to see whether the world is ripe for motorcycles with four cylinders."

As is usual with a Japanese model, the CB 750 was refined with time. In 1971 the CB 750 K 1 came along. The one-into-four throttle cable had been replaced by push-pull operation for the carburettors. (The prototype had featured this system.) The plastic-encased dials were replaced by metal ones. The air filter housing (finished in the colour of the bike) of the first model melted with petrol; the black K 1 item was suitably resistant. The sidecovers were reshaped to make the bike look less massive. The bearing of the output shaft was strengthened. Some other details changed, but major parts were untouched, for the CB 750 was ok from the start. Almost the entire 1969 production was shipped to the USA. In Europe, it was 1970 before we had a chance to buy the model, and in fact it was the next version, the CB 750 K 2, that reached the UK in any quantity. There were control lights on the handlebars instead of in the dials, for the K 2. The headlight shell and stays were black and chrome instead of in the colour of the bike. Many possibly insignificant details were changed, in order to refine the electrics, and the operation of various functions. Colours changed, too. The K 2 was well known for its gold finish; the first series and the K 1 were often red. Other developments were so insignificant that I propose to go on to the K 6. There were countries that never saw a K 3, a K 4 or a K 5. As with so many models, 'development' meant that quality went up as performance diminished. The CB 750, too, followed such a programme, but only to a small degree. A K 6 was 15kg heavier than the first series. It produced some 5 horses less, although the 'claimed' output never changed. Any CB 750 should be able to get 67 horses going, according to Honda!

Then it was 1975 and the CB 750 seemed to be ripe for a successor. A new, more European styling was developed, and the CB 750 F 1 was launched. It was a good-looker, but there were no real technical changes from earlier models. Conservatism! People wanted a four-pipe Honda 750, and the F 1 was no real replacement for the K 6. The K 6 was followed by the K 7, in which the frame was redesigned to enable the bike to be labelled a tourer, not the 'all-round' machine it was before. The cycle parts become larger and heavier, and a fat 4.50 x 17in tyre replaced the 4.00 x 18in rear tyre of the K 6. The four exhausts were redesigned. The whole package looked very like the old CB 750, but in fact only the engine remained the same. In 1977, the competition had caught up with Honda; so the CB 750 F 2 made an appearance. The engine was painted black and it was tuned to deliver more horsepower. Comstar wheels struck a new note. This model was sold until 1980, when all the big makers had fours in every capacity class. People were referring to fours as the 'UJM' – the Universal Japanese Motorcycle. Fours were the cornerstone of the motorcycle world. Funny how things develop in only ten years …

In the seventies it was popular practice to build special versions of Honda's CB 750. The Rickman CB 750 is an example. Handling of the Rickman was better than the original CB.

Honda tried new directions with this version of the CB 750 with torque converter, the CB 750 A Honda-matic. "Gear lever" is a selection handle for urban or open traffic situations. There was no clutch. The blue machine is a 1978 CB 750 A 3, the apple-green one the first version, the CB 750 A 1.

Last of the CB 750 line. The 1978 CB 750 F 2 had increased power to make it competitive against the Suzuki GS 750. Now the Honda was no longer in the lead in the 750 class.

THE SEVENTIES
FROM BIG TO GIANT

In the sixties the Japanese had to fight for their place in the world. They had to prove that they could make motorcycles. After 1974 sales figures go up very rapidly. By then every manufacturer is offering a full-scale model range, from tiddlers to big bikes. Only Suzuki and Yamaha were to face big problems in this decade. They would overcome their troubles, and grow. Almost all the models produced in the sixties are worthy of extensive description whereas the seventies resulted in motorcycles that are much less significant. Not because they were not good: but simply because they do not represent any major development. For example, a Honda CB 360 of 1975 is not at all a bad model, but technically this 'half a CB 750' does not stand in its own right as an outstanding motorcycle – as is the case with a CB 72 or a CB 750. More examples of these so-so bikes? Well, I'd propose: Suzuki GS 400, Kawasaki Z 200 or Z 400; Yamaha XS 360; or Honda CB 200. And if you ask, should I go to the trouble of restoring one of these bikes? my reply would be firm: do so, if you want to, for it's your own opinion of the model that is important. Certainly more important than mine. My choice is usually influenced by the historical or technical impact of a model; yours may be governed by personal memories. Both approaches are OK.

Four-pipe CB 750 K model was supposed to be superseded by the F 1, then by the F 2. But the classic model remained so popular that it stayed around. This is a 1978 CB 750 K 7. It looks much like the old K, but in fact there are many changes.

HONDA IN THE SEVENTIES

Honda entered the 1970s with a full range of models. There were the C 50, C 90, S 90 bikes in the smallest class. There were more, in fact, but those were the most important in the category. The CB and CD 125 were twin-cylinder bikes that looked more modern than the CB 125 SS of the sixties but were, merely, simplified versions of that classic. The CD 125, in particular, was a good, reliable commuter bike. Providing cheap and reliable transport may not be a looked-for feature in a classic motorcycle, yet it is undeniably a worthwhile attribute. The best in this department was the CD 175 that started life in 1967, and grew to great popularity after a 1969 facelift. It was bought by people who had no affinity with motorcycles. They just wanted cheap transport. The 250 and 350 classes were covered by the CB 250 and the very similar CB 350 twins, from 1968. They were built following the technical lead of the CB 450 Black Bomber, but in rather simplified form, having one camshaft instead of two, for example. Styling followed the lines of the CB 750 after 1971. The blue/white or red/white versions of the sixties did have something of an individual face.

The CB 250 G and CB 360 G came along in 1974, and came over as bland and slightly under-powered runabouts. They, in their turn, were succeeded by the CB 250 T and CB 400 T which, apart from their three-valve heads, were of only minor technical interest. In fact the engine was quite gutless. All these models sold in fairly large numbers, as they represented good value for money. The four-cylinder range was extended to the smaller-capacity classes in this decade, when 1971 saw the birth of the CB 500 Four.

This was, technically, a better machine than the CB 750. Details were improved. Mechanical noise was less. The cylinder-head could be taken off without first having to take the engine out of the frame. Production of many components was rationalised, in comparison with CB 750 arrangements. The CB 500 turned out to be even stronger than a 750; not in performance, but in durability. It had a really

(left) In 1971, Honda's four-cylinder motor came down the capacity line. The CB 350 Four followed the styling of the 750, but the engine was even more robust. It was rather simpler, too.

(right) The 500 cc class was not forgotten. The CB 500 Four was made between 1971 and 1975, and was on offer until later; apparently there was a lot of unsold stock...

unburstable engine which, tuned, was able to challenge Kawasaki 500 Mach 3. Styling of the CB 500 was hardly distinctive; it looked like a little CB 750. Even more so after 1973, when the green and black (or brown and black) fuel tank was traded in for CB 750 K 6-like styling.

In 1972 it was joined by the CB 350 four in Europe (but not in Britain). What I've said about the 500 four goes for the CB 350 four. It was very, very tough, but no great performer (the 350 twin was faster). It sounded nice, especially at high revs ...

The CB 350 four was followed by CB 400 and CB 550 fours, in 1974. The 400 became very popular in Britain. The design of the four-into-one exhaust of these models was very much appreciated. However, I repeat: in spite of many good qualities, these models do not represent any major step forward in design, being merely refinements of original CB 750 technology. A marketing failure that is worth mentioning at this stage is the CB 750 Hondamatic. Honda had previously tried Wankel engines but were discouraged early on, and left them alone. Then they turned to automatic transmission. It was believed that, as in the automobile world, there would be people who would fancy easy-to-operate motorcycles, and of course doing away with gear-shifting was an obvious step to take. It was a failure because, simply, people did not like automatic motorcycles. Styling of the auto bike was different from the CB 750, notably with a BMW-like grab rail to the seat. Also, many Gold Wing-like features were incorporated, such as the distinctive front mudguard. Gold Wing-like comfort was there, too. Technically, this was a unique model. Only Moto Guzzi made something similar – and failed to sell their autos, as well. Honda's CB 750 A had a torque converter, combined with low and high gear, low for the city and high for the open road. If you don't want to, you don't have to shift at all. The very smoothly running engine was a detuned and refined

CB 750. Primary drive was by Morse chain, instead of twin chains, which meant, incidentally, that the typical CB 750 chatter was eliminated. The way the power was put to the road was a revelation. It really was a different way of riding; but the motorcycling public apparently didn't feel the need for a change and 1978 saw the end of the CB 750 A.

The 1970s brought other Hondas on to the world stage, notably in off-road motorcycling. There was, in 1971, the XL 250. This little single was, in fact, the first four-stroke off-road motorcycle, yet the honour of introducing a classic in this area has to go to Yamaha, with the XT 500. There was one other development from Honda worth mentioning – the shaft drive CX 500, in 1978. This unorthodox V-twin was overshadowed by the famous CBX six-cylinder, yet it was of unique, interesting construction. Its styling is generally considered ugly now. The 'plastic maggot', or 'slug', as motorcyclists came to call it, was a pushrod four-valver with

CB 400 four was a 1974 successor for the 350. Stylish exhaust down pipes end in a single muffler. This model was very popular in the UK.

inverted heads, arranged to provide more space for the knees of the rider, with the carburettors placed closer to the centre of the bike. (In fact, a set of carburettors from a CB 400 T parallel twin will fit the CX 500 without adjustment.) Performance was surprisingly good. Reliability at first was poor, because of one real teething trouble: the camchain tensioner was too weak, and would break. After this shortcoming was resolved, the second series of this totally new model went on to enjoy a bright career way into the eighties. I think the CX may become a classic; who knows? When discontinued, it soon become evident that it had left an unfilled gap. It was to be several years before Honda had a worthy successor to the CX in the NVT Revere, in the second half of the eighties.

CB X
SIX-CYLINDER MOTORCYCLING

The CB X is the last important Honda of the seventies. The six-cylinder story can be regarded as 'Honda versus Kawasaki, Part Two', and it really deserves (and gets) a separate chapter. The CB X six is the top of the dohc CB series that succeeded the famous CB 750. That bike had already evolved into the RCB endurance racer. In its turn, the racer was the basis for the next generation of four-cylinder Hondas, identified as the KZ and FA Bol d'Or series. The Fours featured four valves per cylinder and two camshafts, with primary and camshaft drive by

Morse chain. The engines were much livelier and produced more power, running very smoothly, with a sharp throttle response. A CB 900 Bol d'Or can, in fact, be seen as a brother to the classic CB X. It was equally fast, without drawing so much attention to itself. The Euro-styling of these models was highly regarded, providing better looks than Suzuki GS or Yamaha XS lines. The sales race was won by Honda. (Kawasaki Z 1000s were more old-fashioned but highly regarded.) The end of the seventies was seen as the period of the four-cylinder motorcycle: the Universal Japanese Motorcycle. If a reproach was intended in that label, it was hardly fair, because manufacturers could not be blamed for making what the customer wanted. However, inspite of their success, the dohc Hondas did not live up to the reputation of the old single ohc models: the engines tired far sooner, and handling was even worse. Therefore, I suggest, there can be no classic status for the second generation of Honda fours.

■ ■ Yamaha in the seventies ■ ■

The turn of the decade signalled the appearance of the DS 7 and the R 5, for Yamaha. They were the best-quality two-strokes in the middle class at that time. I have written of the huge struggle in the sixties; by 1970 Yamaha had won the battle. It was a pity that in the seventies 250s and 350s should no longer figure as importantly as in the previous decade. The 1973 RD 250/350 became more tractable, with reed-valve induction, and the gearbox gained a further ratio, to become a six-speeder (like Suzuki's contemporary T 250/350). Basic construction of the engine did not change, because no changes were necessary, and this was the case when the RD 400 replaced the 350. The stroke altered, of course, but not the engine layout.

The 1970s were the decade of 'bigger is better', but despite this Yamaha's models continued to sell well in the UK. Admittedly, towards the end of the seventies the RD looked a bit outdated, so it was reborn, in 1981, as the 'Elsie' (RD 250 and 350 LC). The lightweight class was represented by the popular moped FS 1 and the race-bred AS 3 (125cc). There was also the CS 2, of 200cc. In this class it was Honda who were top dogs. However, there were all sorts of small single-cylinder off-road bikes from Yamaha that sold well. The DT 125, 250 and 360 (later 400) two-stroke singles were the best, if not the most advanced, in their classes.

The big-capacity class, up to 750cc, was a painful story for Yamaha. Prior to development of the TX

Tribute to the classic RC 164 six-cylinder racer of the sixties: 1978 1047cc CB X. The engineers were free of the usual process of marketing study and cost calculation.

750, a bike that taught many lessons to the world (and certainly to Yamaha!), Yamaha had tried to build a sophisticated two-stroke. It was to be a four-cylinder in-line. A wooden mock-up was constructed, but people would believe Yamaha were serious. Indeed, the GL 750, as it was to be called, never ran. The TZ 700 four-cylinder two-stroke racer would tell a tale to the world later. Another loss was the demise of the RZ 201 Wankel, a twin-rotor rotary engine that was extremely well built – and so nice to look at! It can only be regretted that public reaction at the 1971 Tokyo motorshow caused Yamaha to abandon the Wankel project. There were four working prototypes. Three were scrapped. The fourth is reported to have survived. I haven't seen it, but my source is reliable...

There is a Yamaha model range that started in 1970 and lasted until 1984. The XS 650 has its own chapter. The XS 500 adds up to a difficult story for Yamaha. In the early seventies Yamaha had no answer at all to the Honda CB 500 four, the Suzuki T 500 or Kawasaki's 500 Mach 3. The 1972-introduced XS 500 was, technically, an interesting bike, but drawbacks in styling, performance and reliability prevented it from being successful. The interesting part is that this double over-head camshaft twin had eight valves. This was not all new, of course, for Nourish in the UK made eight-valve heads for Triumph as early as 1968, but Yamaha was the first to have them in serial production. The bland looks of the model amounted to no more than a weak representation of the TX 750 (this illustrious bike has its own chapter). A TX 500 (in the USA) or XS 500 (in Europe) was not a high performer. Cracks would occur in the cylinder head, from spark-plug site to exhaust valves, and between the valves. The problem was never really sorted out; and finally the model vanished. Having said that, I have seen one example really go at a classic racing event! A revelation was Yamaha's 1975 XT 500 single. The big single had not long been declared dead when Yamaha brought out the XT, and started a trend that continues today. (I return to the XT in another chapter.)

The final developments of the seventies for Yamaha were the XS 750 and the XS 1100. After the difficulty with the TX 750 twin, there was a change of company policy at Yamaha. Once, the slogan had been 'Two cylinders are enough'. Now the XS 750 came along, with three cylinders, and shaft-drive. It was aimed at BMW buyers, as a cheap alternative to the bland, but highly valued, Boxers. The objective

might have been achieved if there had not been too many problems with the triple. The cooling was not right; nor was the lubrication system. Performance was not good enough. Styling was neat – but not neat enough. The problems were eventually resolved, but not quickly enough. The 750's successor, the XS 850, was a good machine, with personality, and resolved all of the problems associated with the XS 750. I rode both models in the seventies. An 850 had the 'go' the 750 lacked. And it was technically ok. But it was too late, and the XS 850, like the 750 before it, was discontinued. John Bloor's Triumph triples may be a sign that this decision was taken too early! The last Yamaha of the seventies did not have quality problems, for the huge

People could not believe this bike was real. The fuel-injected four-cylinder two-stroke of 1972 did not make it as a roadster. A few years later, the TZ 700 racer made its début on the track.

(botom) In the 250 and 350cc classes, the 1970 250 Yamaha DS 7 was the best around. Unfortunately for Yamaha, the up-to-350 category was no longer very important.

The 1968 Yamaha DT 1 marked the beginning of the modern lightweight off-road machine. In the USA, especially, the DT 1 made dirt-bike riding accessible to many more people than the heavy British scrambler machines had done.

XS 1100, or XS Eleven, was a very good machine. The four-cylinder four-stroke engine ran backwards, with ignition advance actuated by vacuum. However, this dohc shaft-drive four was soon to be overshadowed by exotics such as the Honda CB X and the Kawasaki Z 1300. In spite of its high quality the XS 1100 just was not special enough. Its successors in the eighties turned out to be very special …

SUZUKI
■ ■ IN THE SEVENTIES ■ ■

Like Yamaha, Suzuki was more or less outclassed by Honda and Kawasaki in 1970, a year when Suzuki sold the T 500 as their biggest bike. The T 250 and T 350 were modernised versions of the famous T 20. The charisma of that model had vanished with the

facelift. These middle-class Suzukis were good machines, but the contemporary Yamahas were even better and looked far more modern, and sold better. The T 125 Stinger is a very nice bike, when we look at it now, being so radically different in styling, and I class it as a real gem. But in its day, people did not

Yamaha was looking for new directions after the launch of the Honda CB 750. The Tokyo motor show of 1971 displayed this twin-rotor RZ 201 Wankel machine. The public was not interested, causing Yamaha to abandon the bike. Technically, and optically, it was a beauty!

really appreciate the (almost horizontal) twin. A 1970 version of the A 100 looked good and sold quite well. There were some more little runabouts from Suzuki, but they did not make much of an impact.

Then, later in 1970, Suzuki announced the machine that would put the firm back on top of the charts: the GT 750. (We will describe it in a later chapter.) Soon after the GT 750 there were GT 380 and GT 550 air-cooled triples, successful competition for the smaller Honda fours. These middle-class Suzukis had style and performance. They were not as wild as Kawasaki triples, but their reliability was far superior. Kawasakis were raw; Suzukis were sophisticated. They also weighed a lot more. Characteristic features were the Ram Air cooling and the three-into-four exhausts.

Honda fours and Suzuki triples came to dominate the market. The T 500 was holding a place in the sales charts, too. The real flagship for Suzuki, though, was the GT 750 'Kettle'. That one and Honda's CB 750 were top of the bill in 1972, the year when the first GTs were sold. The model would hold its high position until 1977, when it was supposed to be followed by the RE 5. That story is outlined in the chapter on the Rotary Engine 5. Suffice to note at this point that Suzuki were almost destroyed by the Wankel. It was fortunate that when they rapidly made a sort of copy of the Kawasaki Z 1, in the shape of the GS 750, the public immediately accepted that bike. The GS 750 was, indeed, a very good motorcycle. As far as inbuilt quality goes, it may even be one of the very best machines of the decade. Yet it was not really special. The styling was bland. The engineering was adapted from the Kawasaki. Performance was good, but not exceptional. Durability, however, was outstanding. And, indeed, it was the saviour of Suzuki. If this book were dealing solely with Suzuki the GS 750

would rank as a very important bike. But in the context of a general history of Japanese motorcycles, the significance of the GS 750 must be seen as limited. And this judgement goes even more firmly for the GS 400 twin that came out just before the 750. This, too, was a good machine, but it had no impact whatsoever.

In the second half of the seventies the two-strokes had faded away, with the exception of the GT 380, which went on until 1980. The T 250 had a successor in the GT 250, and later, the X 7, which absolutely missed the boat! The two-stroke single-cylinder off-road machines also failed to make a mark. These were difficult times for Suzuki. But after the GS 750, the range of four-cylinder four-strokes was extended, with the shaft-drive GS 850 and the GS 1000, in shaft and chain-drive forms. The GS 550 was the saviour in the middle class, selling really well. Like the 750, all these models were excellent machines. They performed well and they lasted apparently indefinitely. The GS 1000 was a great bike, being one of the first Japanese motorcycles that handled well. Like the Yamaha XS 1100, this Suzuki was overshadowed by the Honda CB X and the

The 1976 shaft-drive Yamaha XS 750 triple was aimed at BMW buyers. Twenty years later it might have become popular, but in 1976 the three's success was very modest.

Engine of the GS 750: heavy, but absolutely bulletproof. It can be seen as progenitor of the successful models Suzuki were to produce in the eighties.

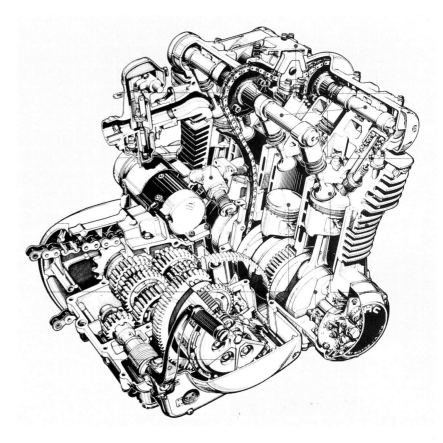

The 1976 Suzuki GS 750 four-cylinder four-stroke was the saviour of the marque after the RE 5 failed as a successor to the GT range.

The 1976 GS 400 twin was perhaps as good as the four, but never received much attention. Yet in 500cc form it is still alive today...

For the Ram Air-cooled GT 380 Suzuki followed the lines of their watercooled GT 750. In order to distinguish their bikes from the Kawasaki 350 and 500 triples, Suzuki increased the engine capacity a little. Hence the GT 380 and the GT 550.

Kawasaki Z 1300. Still, the very conventional Suzuki fours all sold well, providing very good value for money. They were the basis of the success Suzuki achieved in the next decade, the eighties.

KAWASAKI
▨ ▨ IN THE SEVENTIES ▨ ▨

Kawasaki, the aircraft builder, entered the seventies with modernised variants of the Samurai and Avenger twins, and with the 500 Mach 3 triple as flagship. There were, in addition, 90 and 175 singles; but these were not really significant, although performing exceptionally well, with their rotary-disc intakes. They were very tractable, and could keep up with competing machines of greater capacity. Performance really was the key word at Kawasaki. The company had received a blow from Honda with the CB 750, which had caused the Kawasaki 750 four-cylinder four-stroke to be postponed. It was to be the first really sophisticated model for Kawasaki. What happened in 1972 was that Kawasaki brought out the amazing 900 four; but that one will be dealt with in another chapter. In the meantime, a whole range of Kawasaki two-stroke triples took over from the old twins, although the performance of the 250, 350 and 400cc triples was less than that of the twins. But, still, the triples succeeded in Kawasaki's name for high performance – probably, in the main, on account of their thrilling exhaust noise! The raw character of the bikes was an extra attraction for the 'right' sort of people. If you were sports-orientated you could not ride anything other than a Kawa! But as soon as your head took over from the heart, it had to be a Suzuki triple or a Honda four. The worst/best (make your choice) example of Kawasaki's triples, the 750 H 2, is dealt with later.

While Suzuki were searching for alternatives for two-stroke engines, Kawasaki was doing the same. Kawasaki decided far earlier that four-stroke fours and twins were the answer. All the two-stroke makers realised that ever-tighter environmental legislation, especially in the USA, would make life more and more difficult for two-stroke motorcycles. Thus Kawasaki would have the Z 1 (900cc), followed by the Z 400 twin (this latter mediocre machine failing to establish a position in the market). King Z 1 was to be followed by the equally successful Z 1000, which had the looks, and also kept the charisma, of its 900cc predecessor. Performance was a little less; but nobody really cared. This also explains why Kawasaki remained so loyal to the old-fashioned W series (650cc ohv twins) during production of the triples, finally coming out with the Z 750 dohc twin, in 1974. This bike lost the sales battle with Yamaha's TX 750. The Yamaha suffered a lot from technical problems, but looked very good, whereas a Kawasaki Z 750 came over as 'half a Z 1'; and looked it. Technically, it was hardly better than the infamous Yamaha, so there was no real place for the big Kawasaki twin. Nobody seemed to ride it. A pity, because the Z 750 was a touring bike that really had a fine response to the throttle and good handling characteristics.

Then, in 1977, came the Z 650. Technically, again there was nothing new about it, but this bike claimed to combine 750cc performance with 500cc weight and handling. In truth, the claim was not substantiated, but the 650 was still pretty impressive. Together with the Suzuki GS 750, this was one of the best bikes of the seventies, although it hardly rewrote the history books.

YAMAHA XS 650
■ ■ ENGLISH-JAPANESE HYBRID ■ ■

The era of the Superbike had started in 1969 with the Kawasaki 500 Mach 3 and, above all, the Honda CB 750. Suzuki was a little behind at the time, but the GT 750 was in the pipeline. Yamaha missed out on the Superbike boat. It was the XS 650 that gave Yamaha a special place in the market. Not that they did not try to make a Superbike, but Yamaha's trouble was that they did not really know what sort of entry-bike they wanted to make for the new age. There was nothing new for them to produce, for there was a four-cylinder four-stroke on the market, and a two-stroke triple, another logical construction. So they tried a rotary engine. That looked promising in 1969. It was known as the RZ 201, a twin-rotor, and it ran in prototype form. (My judgement is that it was the *rotary* engine that most closely followed the looks of a conventional engine – a notable achievement.) Yamaha were reluctant to try a two-stroke. It was a safe bet that future legislation would make life hard for two-strokes. Yet they built a mock up of a two-stroke four-cylinder… So, what now? Yamaha stepped aside from Superbikes for a while and decided that there might be an interesting market among people who would normally buy an English motorcycle. Everybody knew the virtues of English-type parallel twins. If the – also widely known – drawbacks could be

overcome, there could be a commercial future in bigger twins. The US market was the goal, for there were still a lot of Americans who fancied a big thumper over a sophisticated Superbike. Yamaha had its American marketing people examine what the 'target' people expected. Even details such as the shape of the headlight shell generated extensive correspondence between the USA and Japan. The first study sketches of the proposed bike showed clear Triumph Bonneville characteristics, especially in the outline of the engine, with its upright cylinders and the crankcase. The American market analysts decided that the buyers wanted a modern, slim variant on the Bonneville. When the study progressed, in 1969, the 'Triumph' shapes disappeared from the drawings and were replaced by

Sales brochure for the 1973 Kawasaki 900 cc Z 1. This machine made clear that people were ready for 'more', after Honda's CB 750.

In the USA, the police adopted the Z 1000 as an alternative to Harley-Davidson Electra Glides. The TV series *Chips* contributed to the popularity of this model.

more recognisably Japanese ideas. One thing was clear from the beginning: no absolute copying, of anything, was to be done. There was no need for that, in any case, for Yamaha had done much research work for Toyota in which they had acquired a lot of four-stroke knowledge, even though they had never made a four-stroke motorcycle before. Half a Toyota GT 2000 car engine formed the basic layout of the new Yamaha motorcycle engine. It was a modern engine that was made deliberately old-fashioned in looks. No Triumph part was copied; except for the 'character' of the British bike.

Americans were quite enthusiastic when the Yamaha XS 1 arrived in the USA. The market analysts had been right; this was the machine many people were looking for. The entire production for 1969 and 1970 went to America. In 1971 Europeans received the XS and their reaction was more moderate than the Americans': the bikes were considered to be rather passé. The Dutch, for instance, were far more attracted to Superbikes. The duplex drum brake of the XS 1 was nice to look at, but lacked bite on the road. The XS 1 was soon followed in Europe by the XS 2, which was better received. The 1972 XS 2 had a disc front brake which would stop the bike dead in its tracks, rear wheel aviating. The disc had its own hub, a unique construction that wasn't to be repeated; if play between the disc hub and the hub of the wheel occurred, the disc would rattle when the engine was at tickover. A major complaint of the Europeans centred on lack of an electric starter. Yamaha responded immediately, and the XS 2 was so equipped, in 1972. The starter layout came in at expense of oil capacity in the crankcase, for space needed for the starter motor was taken in the sump, on the underside of the engine. But there were no lubrication problems. The electric starter worked only poorly, and sounded, when actuated, like the proverbial bags of nails. The starter gears wore quite rapidly, and missed gears were often a problem. This was really the only blemish – and, strangely, this starter motor was to be standard equipment on the entire XS 650 series. Even later TX and XV models suffered from inadequate starting arrangements. The parallel twin had a strong, heavy crankshaft carried in four ball bearings. The webs were heavy. Straight primary gears transmitted power to the five-speed gearbox. The clutch was very heavy, requiring a strong left hand to operate it. The gearbox was close to perfection, having, a short-travel, precise control. The transmission was bulletproof. I recall opening

up an Iran police Yamaha which had covered more than 80,000 miles. It was still running on original pistons (although, yes, they were worn). The gearbox really was in as-new condition. Many people, tired of the heavy clutch, would abuse the gearbox by shifting without using the clutch; and always without any observable detriment to the gearbox. The single overhead camshaft ran in four ball bearings, two bearings next to each other, on the ends of the camshaft, with drive by a chain situated in the middle of crank and camshaft. There were two valves per cylinder, operated by hefty rockers.

The engine was very quiet in operation and had, indeed, something of a British quality about it – even to its not inconsiderable vibration, with the front

A few years after the Z 1's arrival, Kawasaki created other four-cylinder models of various capacities. This is the Z 650 C of 1978. Having the weight of a 500 and the performance of a 750, this model enjoyed much popularity.

Yamaha did much development work for Toyota. The Toyota GT 2000 car engine gave its basic configuration to Yamaha's XS 650 unit.

The engine of the 650 cc Yamaha XS 1 was deliberately given a 'British' look. Technically there was no similarity with Triumph, but in road behaviour they were very much alike.

wheel prone to bounce like a BSA's, when the engine ticked over at 400rpm. A beautiful exhaust note added to the fun. From 1,500rpm in fifth gear, when the throttle was yanked open, the bike would take off without hesitation. That is what low-end power is all about. Only a TX 750 had more power available at low revs. Yet if you wanted to ride the Yamaha café racer style, you could do so … The success of this conventional twin encouraged Yamaha to settle on a new company policy. They would forget all about the RZ 201 Wankel and the GL 750 two-stroke. A new slogan was adopted: 'Two cylinders are enough'. The successor to the XS 650 was going to be the TX 750, also a twin, but with more sophistication. In the meantime, the XS 650 was selling well and acquiring a definite following.

However, I have to say that while the 650's engine was good, the cycle parts were a different story. The steering geometry was wrong, and the frame not stiff enough. There had been an effort to keep the bike light; but Yamaha had gone a little too far. Handling was poor, and long, fast corners were to be feared! Speed wobbles, in fact, could happen at quite low speeds. I remember riding an XS 1, and a wobble occurred at 30mph. I did the recommended thing, and slowly increased speed. The wobble diminished. It was easy to maintain the wobble, if desired. That too, was fun on occasions... One could learn to live with an XS 1, warts and all. Still, the general opinion was that XS 1 handling was bad; so something had to be done. But Yamaha did not succeed in sorting out the problems. They called in the British, in the person of road-racer Percy Tait. He had made Triumph Trident racers handle, after they had suffered the same sort of problems that Yamaha was now facing. Tait rode a XS 2 around the block, and reported that the frame should be thrown away! Stiff upper lips at Yamaha… However, they listened closely to Tait's comments. The 1974 XS 650 B (in the USA it was called the TX 650) was given a heavier, stronger frame. The XS 650 would meet European demands as the market there grew. Alloy wheel rims were fitted. The bike gained weight (despite the lighter wheels), but handled better. Styling of the TX 750 had gained favourable comments from the press, leading to a decision that the XS 650 should adopt the same styling. From now on, the XS 650 came over as being far more sophisticated. And this was also a time when the sidecar motocrossers discovered the XS engine, for 1974 had seen a small redesign of the crankpins and the conrods, making them even stronger. The

The XS 1 had a drum front brake that proved inadequate, in spite of its good looks. The 1972 XS 2 was given a single disc up front.

Norton sidecar crossers were soon replaced by enlarged Yamahas of up to 1,100cc, and 100bhp. The engine still kept in one piece!

When the TX 750, intended as a 650 replacement, turned out a failure, it was the old 650 that kept the Yamaha reputation intact. From 1975 on, no real changes to the engines occurred apart from the installation af electronic ignition, dating from the 1978 SE models. The original spark-advance system was of poor quality, but nobody really bothered improving this item, for inaccurate ignition timing never seemed to upset the engine.

In 1976 Yamaha abandoned the 'Two cylinders is enough' concept: they were determined to have a 'Superbike'. Two models were the result. The XS 750 triple was an effort to make a 'slim' motorcycle; but with no real success. Then the XS 1100 appeared, breaking with every Yamaha tradition. This bulky

Encountering a GT 750, you can immediately recognise it by the distinctive radiator.

(right) It's covered 60,000 miles with only minor maintainance. The engine still has its original pistons; speeding tickets were paid; the bike was not spared! This 1975 GT 750 M is still in use today.

(left) Contemporary bikes in comparison. The tuned Suzuki T 500 was faster than the Yamaha XS 2. The latter could be made faster too...

(botom left) Yamaha's XS 650 was available in special police guise. Usually, police machines were white, but the 1975 models that went to the Shah of Iran in 1976 were finished in black.

four was the spearhead of Yamaha's entry into the world of big bikes. Note, though, that these developments didn't prevent the XS 650 from being an important model for Yamaha for quite a few more years. Even the other Japanese makers did their best to bring out versions of the XS 650. Honda tried with a longer-stroke CB 450, giving 500cc. But the CB 500 T vibrated and broke down, frequently. Kawasaki's successor to the W 3, the Z 750 twin, looked too much like a Z 900, and the weak engine helped to kill it off.It turned out that making a good and reliable two-cylinder parallel engine was a tough undertaking … Suzuki would try much later, with the GS 650, which had a reasonable engine, but little charisma. And this was in the 1980s by which time, even for Yamaha, the 'twin-cylinder' period was dead and gone.

At the end of the seventies, Yamaha gave the XS 650 a final face lift. Kawasaki was the first to make what we now know as custom motorcycles. In 1976, Kawasaki brought out 2,000 Z 900 LTDs to test the market. Yamaha was among the followers – and soon was the leading player, for it was found that the XS engine was very well suited to a 'custom' role; even better than a four-cylinder engine, in fact. The 1978 Yamaha XS 650 SE was a fresh entry; even though the engine was dated by then, this model kept the XS

alive until 1983; when production came to an end. By then, sales had slowed considerably, leaving such huge stocks of unsold machines that as late as 1988 it was still possible to buy a new XS 650.

GT 750 SUZUKI
SUZUKI'S ENTRY INTO THE SUPERBIKE WORLD

There are many countries where the Suzuki GT 750 has a nickname: Water Buffalo or Kettle in the English-speaking world; Wasserbuffel in Germany; Boileau (watercooker) in France; and in Holland they talk about Waterorgel or Waterbak (water organ or water can). Two and a half years after the Honda CB 750, Suzuki managed to excite the motorcycling world. The Superbike era had begun with the big Honda and the Kawasaki triples. Actually, Suzuki's contender first turned up in October 1970, at the Tokyo motor show, although this was a little premature, for there was only one show model to be seen, and that one was shipped all over the world during 1971. Suzuki wanted to make sure the world understood that the Honda CB 750 would soon be challenged. Production only started late in 1971 and the first examples, identified as GT 750 J, were sold in January 1972. The introduction had generated

enormous interest in the press, and expectations were high, for the specifications made exciting reading. The Kettle was a three-cylinder two-stroke with a claimed output of 67bhp. (Honda also claimed 67 horses. Coincidence?) The Suzuki was watercooled, however, and this was a real novelty. It is true that in the distant past there had been watercooled motorcycles, but after the humble Velocette LE there had been no serious models featuring watercooling, so in fact it may be said that the Suzuki was the first modern motorcycle to have watercooling. There was a thermo-switch to activate a fan when engine temperature rose too high. But this never happened, for the water pump and the over-engineered radiator were able to keep the engine more than adequately cool. The result was

The Suzuki GT 750 was the first production watercooled motorcycle to be marketed in many years. This one incorporated parts from various years (1972-1977), displaying their interchangability.

that the fan and the switch were simply abandoned in the second series, the GT 750 K. The temperature gauge on the dashboard gave the cockpit a special look.

The Kettle was a very sophisticated motorcycle, with good manners. The front brake was a four-leading-shoe drum which was highly regarded because riders found that it was as effective as Honda's disc brake. (In truth, I'd say it was not really that good!) Race-minded people soon discovered that, as with the T 500, a GT 750 could be tuned and made competitive in racing. The pistons were exactly the same as those of the 500, and porting in the cylinders was very similar. The big Suzuki was even smoother than the Honda CB 750. At equivalent road speeds, the Suzuki could be turning over at 1,000rpm less than a Honda. The engine was rubber-mounted, so no vibration whatsoever was felt. With the bike stationary, a revving engine would dance in its Silentblocs. It was all harmless enough; not even a bulb in the taillight would break. The new constant-vacuum carburettors and the advanced oil injection system, as well as the very neat finish of every part, made the Suzuki a 'gentleman's motorcycle'. But – of course – many people mistook the Kettle for a sports bike, and consequently changed it. Fitting lower handlebars and stripping off parts such as the radiator protector were popular measures. They found it was quite a heavy bike, even heavier, and bigger, than a Honda, which meant that handling was not good enough for sports use. The Formula 1 race bike which tossed Barry Sheene off at 180mph in Daytona had a modified GT 750 engine in a special frame. An extraordinary feature of the GT 750 was its superb reliability: Kettles would keep running even after years of neglect and misuse. The fact that the first series of GT 750 Js had a problem with a water passage in the crankcases, causing coolant to enter the five-speed gearbox, does not invalidate this claim. The problem was solved during production of the J, and even the bikes that gave trouble were easily cured. An extra O-ring between the horizontally split crankcases solved the problem. The GT 750 was and is a unique motorcycle: a two-stroke with the character of a four-stroke, and utterly reliable. You never had to exceed 3,500rpm when riding a Kettle, and full throttle at 1,500rpm, in top gear, was an acceptable ploy. Yet out and out performance was good, with a top speed of 115mph. It would never burst, even when thrashed along on German motorways at full speed. Each year, performance went up a little. If anything critical has

to be said, it's possibly true that the engine was not fond of high revs in a low gear. Electrics were as well developed as the rest of the bike. The Suzuki Recycling Injection System oiling arrangements dealt with any inherent disadvantage of two-stroke mixing.

The model was 'right', from the start, but Suzuki kept refining the bike through the years. The 1973 GT 750 K traded its drum brake for double discs, which meant that the Suzuki would stop at a squeeze of the right hand. Styling was typically 'Japanese', with plenty of candy colours, although it's true that the GT 750 L of 1974 got a more restrained colour scheme, more to European tastes. Port timing was refined, and top speed crept up a little; where Kawasaki triples become tamer with passing years, a Suzuki gained performance. Constant-vacuum carburettors with their central operation helped here, and consumption, too, was vastly improved by the new carbs. The black cones and balance pipes of the three-into-four exhaust system were abandoned, and ground clearance was improved. The frame was stiffened a little, so handling got better as well. In 1974 a digital gear indicator appeared in the cockpit of the GT 750. In 1975 the GT 750 M was introduced; very little change, apart from a less busy paint scheme for the fuel tank. The 1976 model GT 750 A had a cover over the fuel cap, and the tank became rather less bulbous. The gap between first and second gears was reduced. Power was up again, with higher revs. A good GT 750 would touch 125mph.

The last year of production was 1977. The GT 750 B, introduced that year, had improved ignition timing control and the gear change was a trifle better – mainly lighter in operation. Side covers were black instead of in the colours of the bike. The front mudguard of the B can be found on the later GS 750. The Kettle was sold until 1978, when the four-stroke GS took over, definitively. The days of big two-strokes were over. The GT series had taken Suzuki beyond the RE 5 disaster, and the GS series, though not so spectacular as the GT, could carry the Suzuki name to future success. It is fair to say that the Suzuki GT 750 belongs to the little club of best bikes of the seventies. Since 1982 I have regularly used a 1975 GT 750 M. It has clocked approximately 70,000 miles and receives only routine maintenance. The original pistons are still in place. I don't spare the bike: it has to perform as well as my Kawasaki Z 1300! My faithful Kettle still lives up to my expectation today, in the nineties!

This two-stroke engine has a a very gentle personality: it is not the revver two-strokes are generally believed to be.

It produces useful torque from 1,000rpm. Ribbed engine covers are aftermarket items.

The instrument panel of the GT 750, with the temperature gauge in the middle, is still attractive.

This 1972 Kawasaki H 2, or 750 Mach 4, is everything one fears in a two-stroke sports bike. It rattles, screams, revs, guzzles and performs in a very fierce way. Don't be misled by the neat, elegant looks of this motorcycle.

(left) The GT 750, a heavy two-stroke with the road performance of a touring four-stroke, could be transformed into a successful racing machine.

KAWASAKI H 2 750 MACH IV
■ ■ EXCITING; MEAN ■ ■

It screams, it rattles, it smokes, it vibrates and it has a 'rubber' frame. There are virtually no brakes. Meet the classic Mach IV. And maybe become addicted. In 1972 this was the lightest and fastest 750cc streetbike for sale over the counter. Styling was ahead of its time and there was good electronic ignition as standard equipment. At the time Mach IV observers, and occasionally owners, polarised into lovers and haters of the projectile. After the neat and sensible GT 750, it was the alternative that proved Japan could produce a motorcycle with 'character'. As we know, Kawasaki was beaten in the race to introduce a Superbike by Honda's CB 750 four-stroke four. Kawasaki, probably in retaliation, decided to establish a name for pure performance, and the 500 Mach 3 was the first result. The public, looking for speed, was delighted with it; and even more so with the Mach 3 swollen to Mach 4 750cc guise! There were situations on the road in which the 500 had to fight for its place. The speed addicts wanted an outright win, every time. Reliability and finish of detail were of secondary importance. And so, as indicated, to make sure that the world really understood that Kawasaki was into fast bikes, the 750 Mach 4 was brought out. Even though the Z 1 900 was already on its way, this 750, created with such a narrow focus, still ranks as a very interesting motorcycle. The Mach 4 competed against the Honda CB 750, the Suzuki GT 750 and Yamaha's TX 750; perhaps the comparison with the GT 750 seems to make most sense, for both were two-stroke triples – but in fact that is the only thing they had in common. The bikes were opposites. The watercooled GT 750 was a gentle, neat, but also heavy touring machine. If the GT's rev-counter reached the red zone, it meant that the engine had long stopped pulling. Shifting up could be done at 3,500rpm. A Kettle would never surprise its rider. Now, the 1972 750 Mach 4 was air-cooled, which meant an audible ringing of the fins of the lightly built cylinders. The lighting of the Mach 4 was a joke, with its headlight like a candle compared to the Olympic fire of the Suzuki. Accelerating, you had to watch the Kawasaki's rev-counter closely or the needle would pass beyond the red zone while the engine was still revving and pulling! If you weren't alert to this, the engine would explode. Also, you had to watch out for unintended wheelies, even at 75mph! Below 3,500rpm, there was no-one at home in the power department. Things suddenly happened when 6,000rpm came up. Riding at half throttle was no fun. If a Suzuki GT 750 and a Kawasaki H 2 were in company and simultaneously went for it, the Kawasaki would take off as if the Suzuki was at a standstill! Yet on a German no-limit autobahn the Suzuki would be the one maintaining the higher speeds. Detonation with the H 2 would make you shut the throttle. The typical two-stroke surge when the engine hesitates between pulling and decelerating was upgraded to a sort of art on the Mach IV. The bike felt like a bull on such occasions – even worse than an MZ two-stroke single. Engineering tolerances of the Mach IV engine had to be wide and the consequence was that the bike was mechanically noisy. The exhaust note, too, especially on full power, was something again. There seemed to be no 'in between' in the reaction to the Kawasaki:

you either loved it or left it well alone.

The 74 horses ate chains for breakfast in early days, although this was not the Kawasaki's fault, for all new Superbikes suffered from broken chains. It was a typical early-seventies hang-up. Chains improved in quality a few years later, which solved the problem.

The Suzuki triple had a nickname, and the Kawasaki H 2 did too. The Americans called it a Rodeo-bike. This name was not inspired only by the engine's character, for the chassis was not up to the power produced. Weaving and wiggling were commonplace on less than perfect roads. And the bike was light, as well. The front single disc brake was inadequate. Both brakes had to be worked very hard.

▪ ▨ Contrast ▨ ▪

After all this verbal violence about the engineering, perhaps one can be kinder when it comes to describing the H 2's styling. Looking at an H 2 today, it has not aged. The elegant shape and paint does

not look old-fashioned. The slim front mudguard free of stays, the sporty upswept mufflers and the nice tailcover make this bike a good-looker which raises expectations that it will turn out to be a neat and easy-to-ride tourer. This it has in common with the Yamaha TX 750. But the TX fulfils those expectations – not so the Kawasaki! A TX can not run close to 6,000rpm without being in serious danger of blowing up. On a H 2, you have to juggle the throttle as if you were a kid on a moped. Too much throttle and you have an unwanted wheelie; too little and the engine stalls.

In its day, an H 2 would hardly keep running at 1,500rpm. An H 2 weighed only 180kg, while competing machines weighed far more; a Honda CB 750 is an example, at 230kg. In 1973 the Kawasaki's styling was changed, with less pronounced tank lining, and the bike was detuned a trifle: this was the H 2 A. By 1974 the sharp edges of the beast had been well and truly blunted. The engine had been detuned to 61bhp, and it would run at below 3,500rpm, getting seriously out of breath as the red

Drag racing and sprinting were popular diversions for these 'triples with a ripple'. The models aroused mixed emotions. The dragster is a 500, the 750 is good for 7s quarter-mile runs if prepared well.

(top left) **Thumb lever operates the choke. When cold, the engine responds to the choke as if it was the throttle. Once warmed up, the real throttle can take over.**

Tail light cover: all other makes were to use similar covers.

Compare this 750 cc triple engine with that of the Suzuki GT 750. Superficially alike, but basically very different.

line was approached. The 'character' had gone; moved over to the competition.

When the Z 1 came out it did not have to prove that it was fast. That name for speed had already been established, with the triple. The H 2 B frame was strengthened, curing the weave. The single disc brake was doubled up. The 1974 H 2 B was a success, too. The styling, with the big 'Kawasaki' logo on the fuel tank, was very neat, even more so than on the first version. These bikes were bought by hard-core speed addicts – the people who would buy a Suzuki GSX R 1100 in the eighties. The lost horses of the later variants (there had been a 1975 Mach 4, as well) are easily recovered by dint of mild tuning. Nobody should be surprised, even now, to see these machines on the race tracks long after their heyday when they were known as the Green Meanies. The drag strip is another arena of success for these Kawasakis in the 90s, some of them still managing a 7second quarter-mile.

Few H 2s survive to the present day. Inexperienced riders easily got into trouble on them, writing off the bikes (and, sometimes, themselves). Another factor was the prosperity of the seventies, when motorcycles were soon declared out-of-date – obsolete – and consequently were disposed of: a two-stroke more readily than a four-stroke; a Japanese bike sooner than a European machine. The machines bought by the 'wrong' people had the best chance of survival. The sort of people who thought they had bought a neat tourer and then, instead of trading it in immediately after discovery of their

mistake, learned to live with it. Generally, these owners did not put many miles on the clock. A good example is the blue 1972 machine in my collection. The man who bought it back in '72 had mistaken it for a tourer. He used to make one holiday trip every year, of 1,000 miles, together with a friend on a BMW R 75/5. Fourteen years later he sold the bike to his brother-in-law. It was in good condition; a fortnight later, the second owner had a crash on the bike! The damaged bike ended up in his shed, to be purchased by me six years later.

If I have given the impression that riding a Kawasaki 750 Mach IV can be dull – that's misleading! Riding the beast is in fact sheer fun. The hair-raising exhaust music, the moaning of the primary drive, the raw vibration and the adrenaline-raising handling are tremendous. If I feel down and out, the H 2 is good medecine!

YAMAHA TX 750
▪ ▪ 'FOAMBOAT' ▪ ▪

Yamaha's successor to the XS 650 was intended to meet two requirements in 1972. It had to follow company policy of 'Two cylinders is enough'. It also had to be an answer to the Superbike invasion. The TX 750 turned out to be a loser, although it was a valuable exercise in highlighting a technical lesson the entire motorcycle industry was to find of benefit. In 1969 Yamaha had missed their chance to bring out a Superbike. The RZ 201 and the GL 750, described earlier, were going nowhere. Now the

stylists had to find a way to create a particular identify for Yamaha. Their problem was that all types of motorcycle were already on the stocks but manufactured by the 'opposition'. The Suzuki GT 750 was there, and the Honda CB 750, and the Kawasaki Mach 4 – plus BMW's R 75/5. The Triumph Bonneville was a 750 by this time, and

there was the Trident too. Norton was still in the race with the Commando. Laverda and Moto Guzzi were marketing the highly regarded GT and SF and V 7 models. The first Ducati L-twins had been presented to the world. Yamaha's TX 750 was meant to combine the best of both worlds. Alloy wheel rims acknowledged an Italian influence. A double disc at

"Timeless touring" is more relevant today than Yamaha believed in 1973, when the model came out. Nowadays the machine is better suited to its task than in its early days. Motorcyclists of today take it easier.

the front and a huge drum brake at the rear were state of the art. Slim, chromed mudguards added to the modern look – as did omission of the usual fork gaiters. Typical Japanese painting and quality of finish were raised to a higher plane on the TX 750. The quality of switches, dials and fittings was unapproachable. The engine, it was decided, had to be a twin-cylinder in deference to conservative tastes. The TX was to take the place of the 650 after a while, so nil vibration was a mandatory design requirement. Performance had to be up to the standard of other modern 750s. All the 750s of the other makers were closely analysed. The appearance of the engine was considered to be crucial: it had to impress; it had to be modern but, also, sturdy and compact. Style rather took over from function, to the extent that no room was left for an oil-filter! In the end, the oil-filter had to be a very special design and was fitted near the front sprocket. The same sort of situation occurred with the contact-breakers which were, finally, hidden, BSA-like, behind a little cover on the left of the engine.

The engine was to be a twin, but was to behave like a four-cylinder. It even had to look like a four! All this constituted a radical departure from the looks and standards of the XS 650. Technically, the cylinder and head configuration was half a Honda 750, with a single camshaft carried in separate bearing blocks. Oil was supplied from underneath the camshaft carriers. However, the finish of the Yamaha was even smoother than that of the Honda. The bottom end of the engine had no ball bearings, like the XS 650, but shell bearings, like the Honda; the heavy crankshaft was carried in three of these. In order to eliminate the vibration of a parallel twin, the technicians had worked out a system of counter-rotating shafts. Eccentric weights counter compensated for the vibrations of the crankshaft and pistons. Yamaha dubbed the system the Omni Phase Balancer. All this meant that the twin engine was very heavy. The lubrication system was of the dry-sump type – again like the Honda – and was deemed necessary to avoid the enlargement that would have been called for in a wet-sump setup.

The Omni Phase Balancer system worked very well. The engine sounded like a twin but felt, to the rider, like a four. There was absolutely no vibration. That was the good news; but, still, there were major design faults. Those balance shafts were way down in the engine, and oil coming back from the cylinder head was beaten into a froth by the weights, which caused operating temperatures to rise. Froth is not a

DOUBLE DISK BRAKE

(left) The 1974 Yamaha TX 750 tried to combine the super smoothness of a four-cylinder with the manners of a parallel twin. Styling learnt from the GL 750 and the RZ 201 was repeated in this model.

good lubricant! On top of that, the oil circulation system was very lengthy, and complicated, which meant that it took a long time before the oil had passed through the engine. All parts of the engine suffered from a shortage of oil. Another fault was that the main bearings of the crankshaft were not up to their job. There were only three of them, and for a parallel twin ball bearings are more suitable than shell bearings. The engine did not warn when it was over-stressed, apparently revving happily to the red zone of the rev-counter, at 7,000rpm. And the truth was that anything over 4,000 brought problems! Another important aspect concerned the times: in the early seventies in many countries there were no speed limits at all. A Superbike was run at top speed then; as was the TX, because the intention was to turn the TX into a Superbike 750. But, as indicated, this was not to be. As all the problems became evident, Yamaha tried hard to solve them. One 'remedial' service bulletin followed another. Some time in 1973 an unknown mechanic realised that there were oil-cooler sets on the market that might be of use. All machines in stock were modified to take these devices, and bikes already sold were called back to the dealers. Incorporating a cooler meant

(left) Exhaust manifold looked good, but caused the head to overheat. Another nail in the cooling and lubrication coffin of the Yamaha TX 750...

Extension of the cranckcase to allow more oil to be carried was the result of experience of using balance shafts. Thanks to the TX 750, many of today's machines use balance shafts for vibration-free running.

that the oil system was now even more complicated. Two pipes to and from the engine passed behind the air filter and under the fuel tank to the oil-cooler. Often Chausson coolers, intended for Citroën cars, were used, positioned under the steering head. It was a neat modification. But people had lost confidence in the Yamaha, and were not happy. Then, in 1974, Yamaha brought out their own oil-cooler, but made the modification very visible. Two chromed hoses went on the right side of the cylinder block towards the oil-cooler, all in view. The modification certainly helped to make the TX more usable, although full-throttle work was still out of the question. If you stayed below 4,000rpm, the bike was perfectly serviceable; 4,000 in top gear equated to 75mph. Keeping to that sort of performance, the

TX would ran to 60,000 miles without any trouble. But the bike could not live up to the 'Superbike' description; it was a good tourer. The public was not impressed, and 1975 saw the end of the TX 750. It was then the smaller two-strokes and the XS 650 that kept Yamaha afloat – not forgetting the XT 500, of course.

Riding the TX

I write in the present tense, as a present-day TX rider … There is no decompressor, such as the XS 650 had. The 100cc-larger TX engine takes even more effort to start: the starter motor gets the job done. but moans about the hard work it has to do, and I have to say that the kickstarter is the better alternative, even if it takes all one's weight to

Much effort was expended in giving the TX a smooth look. However, under the shiny engine covers things were really complicated...

Top of the bill for the happy few: the 1973 900 cc Kawasaki Z 1 created a sensation. Its nickname 'King' was coined by the public and was taken over by the press, then by Kawasaki.

overcome compression. A good,'heavy' sound is heard as the engine ticks over at 800rpm. Power starts at 1,000 and you can shift up at 2,500. Let it come down to 1,000 in top gear and open the throttle, and the bike will take off without hesitation. The seat is rather high, like that of a Honda CB 750 K 2. And, also like the K 2, this Yamaha has a high centre of gravity. Operating the clutch takes a lot of effort, recalling memories of Laverda twins. Riding the Yamaha, everything is in the right place and one can ride for a long time without getting tired. Gear-shifting has not deteriorated after all these years; and the transmission works perfectly. The TX is a little heavy in the corners; you need to force it a little – like a Laverda. it never wiggles or weaves. On the straights it runs like a train. As I've indicated, fast road work is not the Yamaha's main strength. It will reach 110mph, and at that speed it is free of vibration. But low-down power is the chief virtue of the TX. Treat the TX 750 like a British twin, and you can be very happy on the Yam. Oddly, the 1990s are far more suitable for the TX than was its own era, for nowadays we can't indulge in full speed all the time. Legislation and 'social acceptance' don't allow it. If you want to go fast, take a modern motorcycle.

Modern oil stays up to 30° cooler in the TX and is also more resilient to frothing. The result is that lubrication problems are more or less a thing of the past. The brakes of a TX 750 were excellent for its time, and even today we can judge them as being adequate, or even good. And a TX most certainly is a looker!

The lessons taught by this model are still being put into practice today; many motorcycles now have balance shafts...

KAWASAKI 900 Z 1 SUPER FOUR
■ ■ THE KING STRIKES BACK ■ ■

Kawasaki Heavy Industries was taken by surprise when Honda brought the CB 750 to the world in 1969. It was just the sort of bike Kawasaki had under development! They were, privately, very upset. It took them three years to strike back, with the Z 1 Super Four (also known as Pilot) which set new standards. We have already seen that Kawasaki had soldiered along in the market place with the W 1, in the sixties. Then they brought out the Samurai. The 500 Mach 3 was the first real step on the way to the Z 1. The two-strokes were intended to establish Kawasaki's name as a manufacturer of fast motorcycles. In retrospect, it's probably the case that when Honda came out with the CB 750, Kawasaki should have brought out their four as well. But at the time, Kawasaki thought they did not dare take the risk, believing that only an upper layer of society would be able to afford such an advanced machine, of the standard archieved by such as MV Agusta with the 600 Bialbero, and the rare Münch Mammut, with its NSU car engine. Apart from being hardly obtainable, those sure cost *money*! Otherwise, one saw four-cylinder motorcycles only on the circuits… Benelli, MV and Honda racers, in the main.

With the CB 750 on the market, Kawasaki engineers had an example to study. They didn't copy it, however. A Kawasaki 900 is built absolutely differently from the Honda. Starting with the engine, capacity was increased to 903cc. The bearings of the crankshaft were ball bearings, with needle rollers for the mains and big-ends. Honda used car-type liners and a one-piece crank; a Kawasaki's was of built-up type. Honda's primary drive was by twin chains, Kawasaki used straight-cut gears (responsible for the typical whining sound). A CB 750 had a single overhead camshaft; Kawasaki went for dohc. A Honda cam ran in separate carriers, where Kawasaki used replaceable liners. This was a real

The Kawasaki Z 1 engine (only the 1973 version was black, later they were unpainted) was a four, but it was built in an entirely different manner from Honda's CB 750.

The Z 1 had a single front disc; a second was available, however. Double overhead camshaft operation was to become commonplace on fours.

touch of extra quality. Later motorcycles would have their cams running durably in the alloy of the head. One of the major drawbacks of the Honda was the impossibility of taking off the head without removing the entire engine from the frame. By contrast, using only a few spanners would suffice in dismantling a Kawasaki. The engine carried the oil in the crankcase, unlike the Honda. And the unorthodox Honda gearbox had a very straightforward competitor in the Kawasaki arrangement: the gears of a 900 could easily be used in a Sherman tank! A Honda engine is heavy; to lift a Kawasaki engine you need a crane. In short, both Honda and Kawasaki are fours; but they have very little in common. But both engines are strong and durable; and their quality set new standards.

■ ▩ Styling ▩ ■

The Honda also served as a starting point in establishing the looks of the Kawasaki. Again, the Honda was not copied, but taken as a starting point. The Kawasaki made the Honda look almost old-fashioned. There were four exhausts. That could not be avoided, since it was clear that people wanted them. Their styling was even more eye-catching than the Honda's. There was a disc brake at the front and

a big drum at the rear; with the right fork slider prepared to take a second disc; these brakes were so new that Kawasaki considered it enough to offer a second disc only as an option. The mudguards went a further step forward in styling, losing supporting stays. Ten years later all makes would have mudguards styled like the Kawasaki's. The taillight was integrated into the tailcover. Another styling move that would become widespread.

Honda more or less tried to hide the size of their motorcycle by using a relatively small, short fuel tank. And the overall styling of the CB 750, apart from the candy colours, was mild. Kawasaki, on the other hand, really went to town with a stretched, bright-coloured tank with continuation of the colours in the tail section emphasising the styling. The Z 1 was, unsurprisingly, fast, although it was in fact little ahead of the 750 Mach IV. There was an important difference, however. The 750 was a real gas guzzler and gave its rider a feeling that it might break down, any time! The big four-stroke, by contrast, seemed and was unburstable. It had good road manners. It was easy on fuel. After a one-hour full-speed run on German motorways, a Z 1 would happily tick over at a standstill. It turned out to be a good move to go up from 750cc, lifting the Z 1 above the ruck represented by Honda CB 750, Suzuki GT 750, Yamaha's TX 750, BMW R 75/5, Laverda 750 SF, Moto Guzzi V 7 Sport. Even the British had 750s in the lists, with the BSA/Triumph triples.

High over all these ruled the King of the Highways, the Zed One. There was one other 900cc motorcycle, BMW's R 90 S, but that one was far more expensive than the Kawasaki and appealed to a very different group of people. As with Honda in 1969, in 1972 the Kawasaki sold like hot cakes. Finally, Kawasaki was on the map!

There were teething troubles with the King, albeit of a minor nature. Occasionally, a crack in the cylinder head would develop between the exhaust valve and the spark plug, generally caused by taking off at full throttle on a cold engine. Another snag was that the rotor of the dynamo, being rather weakly constructed, would sometimes explode! As soon as this was noticed, the rotor was improved in production. The last minor, though bothersome, weakness was the bike's voltage regulator, in which current ran too high, causing bulbs and even ignition coils to give up. This took a while to be sorted out. But these little inconveniences, and they were not much more than that, did not prevent the

Second version of the Z 1 was the 1974 Z 1 A. Castings were thicker for better damping of engine noise. Staight-cut primary drive, cam chain and roller crankshaft bearings caused the din.

engine from archieving a high reputation for strength and durability. The Kawasaki was to be the basis of many drag racers, which are the sort of motorcycle that expose the limits of what an engine can take. Drag racers are bored out, tuned, supercharged. The most exotic fuels are used. Some engines are tuned to put out more than 200bhp... The 1973 Z 1 was unaltered from the previous year. The line was joined by a series of police models that made their name in the US television show Chips. More and more police forces in the USA adopted the Kawa as their workhorse; but not in Britain, where the police turned to BMWs. The Japanese home market had a restriction of 750cc in those days. So the 900cc Kawasaki was brought down to 750cc for home consumption. Funny people, the Japanese... The 750cc Z 2 was exactly the same as a 900, but with altered bore and stroke sizes. Very few of these 750s made it to Europe.

In 1974 the first real model change took place, when the Z 1 A appeared with an unpainted engine instead of the all-black finish of the first Z. The

crank was heavier and the engine castings similarly more massive. Measures had been taken to dampen out internal engine noises. The heavier crankshaft and the smaller carburettors (26mm instead of 28mm) made the engine a little smoother. So the Kawasaki did not suffer from the changes; but in fact gained in sophistication. The real background was that handling was not as good as engine performance. Some riders had got themselves in trouble riding hard – the drop in power cured this problem! The styling was also, to my mind, a small step backward, with the fuel tank being adorned with extensive lining. In 1975 the oil drip-feed on the left side of the bike was omitted, which meant that a little oil tank and an adjustable nozzle, to oil the chain, were struck off the specification. Drive chain in those days had had a hard life coping with 82bhp, but any oil supply to the chain meant that the left exhausts became very dirty. The following year, 1976, was the last season for the 900. Styling had become very restrained as the sporting role of the model was traded in for a more touring-oriented appeal. Performance was down again, but nobody seemed concerned. A 1973 Z 1 had been much faster than a 1972 Suzuki Kettle; by 1977 the Suzuki could outperform a Z 900.

Quite separately from regular Z 900 A 4 production in Kawasaki's American plant, an experiment was carried out to arrive at the Z 900 B2, better known as the KZ 900 LTD. This was the first custom bike as we now know them. Kawasaki wanted a piece of the action from Harley-Davidson and Moto Guzzi, after noting that Harleys and Guzzi Californias appealed to an entirely new kind of customer. Two-thousand Z 900 B 2s were built in 1976, and the experiment proved a success, for the model was well received. Strangely, though, after the first 2,000 no more B 2s were built until 1978, when the next series appeared in the form of the Z 1000 LTD. The other manufacturers had discovered this market as well, by 1978, and indeed, the Yamaha XS 650 SE was an even more notable example of the custom form than the Z 900 LTD.

In the USA custom bikes soon came to form the major part of the motorcycle market. The 1976 Z 900 was followed by the 1976 Z 1000, the models looking very similar. The 1000 merely traded a little top speed for additional tractability. The bike was aimed at the tourer rather than the sportsman. In 1978 the 'opposition' came up with an answer, with, for example, the Suzuki GS 1000 proving an even better motorcycle than the Kawasaki 1000; but charisma and fame kept the Kawasaki ahead of the Suzuki. The Yamaha XS 1100 displayed the heritage of the TX 750 and the XS 750 triple, but that was not a recommendation in 1977, when the XS 1100 came

out. Honda did not, apparently, have an answer to the Z 1000; and yet, in fact, it did. The CB X six really outclasses the Z 1000, but the more 'normal' models, like the CB 750 and 900 Bol d'Or, were not up to challenging the big Kawasaki (or the Suzuki GS 1000). In any case, Kawasaki's answer to Honda's six was the Z 1300 six.

Kawasaki's Z 1000 range went on and on. In 1978 a new model was put into production. This was the Z 1 R, with slim lines and a nice handlebar fairing. Towards the end of the seventies the Z range was even further extended with the Z 650 four, mating a a 500's weight with 750-class performance, according to Kawasaki. The Z 650 found many happy followers. The Z 500 four was a good machine, too, but was lost in mists of anonymity. The 1000cc range was widened: the Z 1000 ST was a shaft-drive version of the Z 1000.

Into the eighties, and the range went on. The excellent GPz 550, 750 and 1100 bikes, that carried on to 1984, were descendants of the Z 1 of 1973. But in 1983, with the birth of the GPZ 900 R (note the difference in writing; this is no typing error), a new era began.

Riding today

A Z 1 was a large motorcycle, although its wide handlebar made it easy to handle, and the seat was not as high as that of a Honda CB 750. As it was a bike of the seventies, there was a kickstarter, in addition to the electric starter. The engine was quiet for its time (though one wouldn't say that of it now, judging by contemporary, 1990s, standards). With choke on, the engine did not immediately fly up to 6,000rpm, as later Kawasakis tended to do. The Z 1 ticked over gently, and gear-shifting and brakes all felt good. The engine reacted slowly to the throttle – the effect of a heavy crankshaft and huge clutch drum. The brakes were not particularly powerful. The note of the four separate exhausts was quite undistinctive, improving a little as revs climbed; later machines sounded rather better.

In 1973 the Z 1 was no less than superb! In fact, I'd say that even today the Z 1 has lots of so-called street cred. I once compared an original 1974 Z 1 A with a 1994 Zephyr 750, for a motorcycle magazine. The modern Zephyr did everything just a little better … (Handling and braking were much better!) Nevertheless, the Zephyr was not that much more of a motorcycle, to tempt one to trade in a real Zed One.

In 1984 nobody used the word 'classic', and the 900

The 1976 Z900 LTD was the first Japanese custom bike. It was the result of an experiment by Kawasaki's American plant. Only 2000 were built. They were a big hit; two years later all the makers would start building machines like this one.

was merely an old bike that could still keep up, more or less, with newer models. They usually consumed a lot of oil but they never broke down – which of course is why a relatively large number have survived to this day. Now we can reasonably call the Zed One a classic. They can still be ridden daily – but be careful with the exhausts, because replacement ones are hard to find nowadays. (Even late seventies owners who changed the bike's four exhausts for a four-into-one system, and put the originals in the attic, will have disposed of them by now.)

SUZUKI RE 5
▧ ▧ A ROTARY ALTERNATIVE? ▧ ▧

Suzuki had made a good start in the Superbike era with their GT 750, as we have seen. But a good start does not mean that the race is won, and in this case there's the RE 5 to prove the point. The GT 750 was a two-stroke triple, and when it came out the crystal ball owned by all motorcycle manufacturers was already showing future legislation on exhaust emissions. For Yamaha, that was one of (many) reasons for dropping the GL 750 two-stroke four, in 1971; Yamaha still had to learn some hard lessons with the TX 750.

Suzuki had a little more time, because the GT was so successful. But instead of cashing in on this success, Suzuki were to come near to bankruptcy in planning their follow-on model range. The company was not enthusiastic about building the four-cylinder four-strokes which the market seemed to demand. They felt a Suzuki four would not be distinctive enough to be a worthy successor to the famous Kettle. And, also, the early seventies was a

period when much interest was being shown in Wankel engines. Mr. Felix Wankel was the inventor of the rotary engine, and his fellow countrymen at Sachs and NSU in Germany seemed to be on the road to success with their motorcycles and cars using the Wankel engine. Almost every manufacturer of the time, not only the Japanese, was experimenting with rotary engines. BSA, and later Triumph, had a rotary on trial in 1969 that would eventually see life as the Norton Commander of the eighties. Another example was the German Hercules (or, in some countries, DKW) W 2000. I have ridden one, and found it a lovely bike; but it wasn't a success. Mr. Van Veen of Holland made his OCR 1000 out of a BMW-framed, Mazda-driven prototype, in 1974. An OCR 1000 is an expensive classic nowadays (almost all 30 bikes built by Van Veen are in the USA now). Even MZ, behind the then Iron Curtain, toyed with Wankel. Last, but not least, the Russians tried Wankel engines.

Everybody experienced severe problems with the rotaries, but Suzuki thought they would eventually overcome all the troubles. They had a contract with NSU and Mr. Wankel himself, and all were pledged to help on a communal basis in sorting out technical hitches. One after another, the other makers abandoned the rotary – most even before rideable models were tested. Honda had a little rotary engine replacing the cylinders and pistons on the base of a CB 200 twin. Yamaha had the RZ 201, as mentioned earlier. Still, Suzuki persevered, building a new factory to produce the engines. A system of rotary replacement was thought out: motorcycles with engine trouble would not be repaired at a dealer; instead, the dealer would take out the engine and send it to Suzuki's special department, in exchange for a re-conditioned unit to install in the bike. Another department would then re-condition the incoming defective engines.

Styling was to be distinctive, so Italian designers were invited to submit drawings. 'Italian' influence was manifest in the use of alloy wheel rims and rimmed mudguards, and completely round winkers. The lining on the fuel tank was unconventional. However, the most distinctive gimmick defining the looks of the bike was neither 'Italian' nor 'Japanese'. I'm referring of course to the hood over the futuristic-looking dials. When the ignition key was operated the hood sprang open – that is, if you had remembered to close it by hand when previously parking the bike. The hood was absolutely useless, but everybody who's ever seen a Suzuki R(otary)

(right) **Blue-finished machine is the 1976 RE 5 A, the red one is from the first series (1974, 1975).**

This shapeless lump of alloy is an engine. The Suzuki RE 5 unit was built in cooperation with NSU of Germany. This fact was noted on the castings of the engine (near the spark plug).

E(ngine) 5 will remember it! The other thing that will be remembered is the audible beep, emanating from an ignition condenser. The ignition setup of an RE 5 was a points unit combined with an electronic device.

The new series of models was to put Suzuki ahead of everybody at a stroke. That was the intention, anyway. Every technical magazine was intensely interested in the Wankel engine. It was widely believed that the rotary stood a good chance of replacing the reciprocating-piston engine altogether. Problems with rotor seals and the high fuel

consumption were expected to be overcome …
The RE 5 was to be only the first of a whole range of
rotary-engined machines. The single rotor of the 5
could be doubled to a 10, or tripled to a 15, which
would grace a 1500cc bike! Suzuki were attempting
nothing less than a whole new technology in
motorcycle manufacture.

So the RE 5 was announced in a blaze of publicity,
in 1974, as the bike for the *eighties*. The press loved
it. Tests were carried in independent magazines, and
the disadvantages, like the enormous thirst and the
mediocre performance, were made light of. Almost
every reporter was thrilled with the bike. This is
easy to understand: if one sees motorcycles every
day, and has tried everything on the market, one
tends to look for something really new. But the
public did not share the enthusiasm. For the
ordinary rider, the RE 5 came over as far too
futuristic: the Honda CB 750 was revolutionary
enough, thank you very much! The winkers and
hood over the dials were considered ugly. And there
was 'no engine – just a lump of alloy'.

Soon, there was no talk from Suzuki of the RE 10
and the RE 15. Even the RE 5 cost more than a
GT 750, and gave slightly less power. The fact that
that power was churned out in such an agreeable
way did not impress. The weight was high up, so the
handling felt different. Not precisely bad; but
different. Reaction to the throttle was also very
different from that of a normal bike. The first three-
quarters movement of the twistgrip operated only

(top left) **Too advanced
for 1974: the dials
would be acceptable
10 years later. The RE
5 was advertised as
"the machine for the
eighties"...**

(top right) **Alloy rims,
slim mudguards,
rounded winkers:
features of the Suzuki
RE 5.**

**The remarkable RE 5
tail light was replaced
by a GT 750's in the
second series, the RE 5
A. Ten years on, it
would have been quite
acceptable.**

the two small primary intake ports, which meant
there was little engine response. When the vacuum
box on the carburettor opened the big secondary
port, the real work began. All this meant that when
the rider was changing gear, the throttle was not to
be closed. You had to keep it three-quarters open.

An RE 5 really is something 'different' to ride...

People never got used to the technique. On the other hand, a decelerating engine had hardly any braking effect. One had to learn how to ride again! People were not prepared to do that, and the result was that hardly any RE 5s left the showrooms.

For 1975 the model was adapted a little, with a more conventional styling. The taillight from the GT 750

was taken over and the futuristic meters and the hood were replaced by the arrangement familiar from the GT 750 B (though they were not exactly the same, as many people think). Throttle response was improved. All to no avail. Nobody wanted the Wankel. Suzuki's huge investment had been for nothing; 1976 saw the end of the model and Suzuki gave up on rotaries. An old trick from the fifties was employed at this critical juncture. Look out for a successfull model - and copy it! The Kawasaki Z 1, the 900, was taken as the bike to follow. A GS 750 is very Kawasaki-like. It is (even more so than the Z 1..) a very, very good motorcycle. And people accepted it as such. The GS 750, and the GS 400 twin that went with it, saved the company. In fact, it was the basis of the 16-valve GSX 750 and 1100 of the early eighties that were to carry Suzuki to great heaghts.

So the RE 5 had its... shortcomings. Yet there are examples to be found that have clocked many, many miles. They suffered a lot of failiures in early days with the specially designed NGK AUI 10 EFP spark plugs. These plugs cost a fortune when they were available; if you sell one now, you can make an auction of it! Mechanically, a rotary Suzuki never breaks down. Some have made world trips, including crossing the Sahara desert. My own RE 5

is such a Sahara veteran (but certainly not the only one). When I purchased the bike, it had 80.000 miles on the odometer. At low revs one could hear the rotor wiggle over the eccentric shaft. It was a bad starter, but it always finally burst into life. Now one of the very last re-conditioned engine units is waiting for installation in the bike...

■ ■ Riding the RE 5 ■ ■

There is a kickstarter, but it could have been omitted, with no loss. When cold, the engine can not be started on the kickstarter; warm, and using your whole weight, you might just succeed in overcoming the compression and then, if you are lucky, it will start. Fortunately, there is an electric starter. It makes an audible effort of the job; but it works. Of course, this is not a four-stroke, and nor is it a two-stroke. The exhaust note is almost indescribable: a deep, dark, sharp noise, combined with a whine from the side seals in the engine. A GT 750 with one of the

The 1974 500 cc Suzuki RE 5 was meant to be the first of a complete line of rotary-engine motorcycles. But this whole new direction in motorcycle construction was soon abandoned. Italian styling influences can be traced in the RE 5.

four battle pipes removed comes close to giving an RE 5-like note. The rhythmical 'skipping' of the ignition when one is decelerating is a joy to the ear. Getting under way, a heavy crunch will confirm that first gear has been engaged but later, as long as the throttle is not closed, the other gears are more easily engaged – even without the clutch, if you so wish. Acceleration is very smooth from 2,000 to 5,000rpm. Beyond 5,000, it becomes rocket-like and if you don't watch out, it passes smartly through the red zone on the rev-counter, probably until it explodes which is what we said about Kawasaki triples; remember? Yet the RE 5 feels so different from the Kawa triples, the Suzuki being much heavier, and more sophisticated. No vibration is felt with the RE 5 (a Kawa triple vibrates heavily when revving). Only under 1,500rpm, in a yellow zone on the rev-counter, is the engine unhappy; in the middle revs range, on the last quarter of throttle opening, the response of the RE 5 is marvellous. The riding position is very comfortable and the brakes, the same as on the later GT 750s, are good. The high centre of gravity does not bother the rider. Cycle parts are improved GT 750 items, which means they are really impressive. Fast cornering is a doddle on a Wankel. Top speed is 110mph, and the bike feels ok when cruising at 85 – 'all day' if you want to … lack of fuel-tank capacity will make you stop, not your aching back! However, if you amble along, the engine may skip a beat or two. Then it has to be revved hard in order to clear the plug: compare it to a slow two-stroke with racing plugs … But as I've said, be careful with the plug; there is only one, and they are no longer available.

It is a special feeling to be on the road with such an unorthodox engine. Anyone who can say he rode an RE 5, or has even heard one, may think himself privileged. Suzuki was nearly killed off by the minimal sales of the bike; but, still, it is a real classic! Suzuki should have been awarded a prize for enterprise, at least.

The rotary engine is not dead. Mazda has dominated some classes in sportscar racing since 1980 with modified rotary RX 7s, and aircraft and snowmobiles are equipped with rotaries. Perhaps in the future, with ceramic materials that could ease the cooling and lubrication problems, the rotary might become commonly viable.

YAMAHA XT 500
■ ■ UNEXPECTED TREND-SETTER ■ ■

So far, we have been involved in the so-called Superbike era. We have also seen that Yamaha had a bad commercial period in the big-bike field, with the TX 750. One of the pillars on which the recovery of Yamaha was based was the 500cc single, which of course barely qualifies for 'classic' status. The XT 500 can be seen as marking the start of the off-road phenomenon.

In 1975, the single-cylinder four-stroke motorcycle was, more or less, extinct and buried. The last spectacular big single had been the Velocette Venom Thruxton, a classic made until 1971 – though of course in very small numbers. Then the Goodman family at Veloce Ltd simply stopped making motorcycles. The design of the Venom dated back to the 1940s. Another well-known single was the BSA

Behind the cover is the primary chain; behind the rotary-shaped emblem, the clutch.

DBD 34 Gold Star. Production of this model had stopped even before the Venom's end. Nevertheless, there were a few singles around in 1975; for instance, Honda's XL 125 and XL 250. But they went relatively unnoticed. The other makers had 250, 350 and 400cc two-stroke singles with high mudguards which were in the main (very) tame motocrossers made suitable for the road. Nice to play with; but no more than that. Certainly there were no mainstream models.

And then, suddenly, there was the XT 500. A thoroughly modern four-stroke single engine delivering relatively good power was housed in a bike that could be used on dirt. It was easy to ride as it wasn't so 'nervous' as the two-strokes. But it had more power than the Honda four-strokes. It sported full equipment for the road: good lighting, winkers it was all there. This was a bike that could actually be ridden to the track, on the highway. You could have a good day out scrambling, and then motorcycle home.

The press misunderstood the XT at first. Many reporters wrote about the revival of the single, as if the Gold Star and the Venom now had a ready-made successor. No way; those classic English bikes were serious sports (read: near-racing) bikes for fast cornering on the road, and they were ridden by very different motorcyclists from XT people. Having said that, I will admit that BSAs were also used in various events in the dirt, but never on a big scale, simply because not many dirt-suitable Gold Stars were built. And BSAs were expensive. The widely available XT 500 opened new paths in an ever-growing motorcycle world, and a new kind of motorcyclist bought them. There was no better bike for crossing the open American deserts than this Yamaha. Before, it had been a matter of using modified motocross machines from the European makers, like Maico, Husqvarna, Penton (KTM), Bultaco and others. Or old Triumph and Norton twins. It took tough men, and women, to ride those sorts of bikes. Now the XT 500 made the achievement easier, and the desert was open to more people. Globetrotters discovered the Yamaha. They had a choice, instead of being 'sentenced' to a BMW! Not much of the past had rubbed off on the Yamaha XT 500, as far as engineering was concerned. The engine was a very compact unit with a stiff crankshaft carried in large ball bearings. A lightweight, shallow piston ran in an alloy-finned cylinder. The cylinder had a single camshaft, with drive by chain. Two ball bearings kept the cam in its

place. There were two valves and the engine was a high revver; bore and stroke were 87 x 84mm. Lubrication was dry sump with the frame serving as a reservoir for the oil, which allowed the engine to be positioned higher in the frame, giving more ground clearance. Omission of an oil tank meant that the bike could be a little slimmer. Only one aspect was reminiscent of old, modified competition bikes: the electrical system was only 6 volts, with ignition fed directly by coil and flywheel, the little dynamo supplying the battery, and the rest of the electrics energised by the battery.

Detail finish was not as sophisticated as on the road-going motorcycles, but was neat and practical. The 28.5bhp XT was fast enough for road use; it wasn't particularly comfortable, but it would run at 85mph without tiring. The engine could be tuned to deliver much more power than standard, but then rideability on the road was in jeopardy.

The whole concept was right, first time out. And the electrics were not bad enough to be a real problem; most people got rid of the winkers and the big street taillight, anyway. A smaller headlight and a tiny taillight were considered adequate by most riders. The enormous exhaust system was changed by many owners. The downpipe passed underneath the engine, to end in the first muffler, which was situated behind the right damper. This first muffler ended in a second one, high up at the right side of the bike. In 1977 Yamaha made a change here: the downpipe

Off-road bike that brought back the big four-stroke single: this is the 1976 Yamaha XT 500. It was to remain in the sales lists until 1989.

Lightweight drum brake on the front wheel of the XT 500 struck an odd note in the era of disc brakes.

was altered to follow a pattern we have seen earlier when, like a BSA Victor, the pipe went alongside the engine into the modified first damper. The better, and visible, engine protection shield made the bike look far lighter.

The difficult starting procedure – the engine would kick back if the kickstarter wasn't operated with sufficient force – was eased a little by siting a little peep hole in the camshaft housing. A pointer would indicate when the cam was in the right position for starting. A hand-operated decompressor made finding the optimum position possible. It took a few

years, but then the other makers discovered that the concept of the XT 500 was here to stay. So they came out with competing machines; Honda with the XL 500. Technically, this was a far more advanced machine. The kickstarter was abetted by an automatic decompressor that worked really well. People with no 'kickstarting' background could start it. Four valves gave the Honda a more modern specification than the XT, but still it did not succeed in trampling on the XT. Suzuki, however, had rather a bad experience with their SP 370. It didn't look right, and didn't perform well. Kawasaki, too, made an effort, with the KL 250 and later with the KL 500. But finally it was Yamaha itself that challenged the XT 500, with the more modern XT 550, that had all the answers for the Honda as well. The later XT 600 and the XL 600 were followed by more variants. Suzuki and Kawasaki managed to catch up, more or less, as the off-road sector became a major division in the motorcycle world. The old XT 500 remained immensely popular. Never mind its better, faster, more sophisticated successors. The first rally from Paris to Dakar was won on a XT 500, which gave it enduring status. The engine's sub-30bhp power was not, of course, enough for real racing. Many tuners succeeded in making the bike give 45 to 50bhp. For competition purposes, the engine was reliable enough.

The first XT500 carried the exhaust under the frame, causing the right shock absorber to overheat; from 1977, the pipe passed behind the side cover.

Tuned XTs with their high suspension did not shine in motocross but they lasted well and were highly appreciated by many. 'Leisure-time' scramblers loved the bike! Much later, the European makers such as KTM and Husqvarna built competitive four-strokes for motocross. They owed something to the old XT 500. Enduro racing was different. Here the Yamaha TT 600 and the Honda XR 600 became dominant – the Honda especially.

The XT went on sale in 1976, and survived beyond most of its competition; as late as 1990 the last XT 500s were sold. A 1990 XT can be parked next to a 1976 or 1977 model, and only minor details differences will be apparent. Surely the XT 500 deserves to be remembered as THE off-road bike of post-war years?

HONDA GL 1000 GOLD WING
▪ ▪ IN A CLASS OF ITS OWN ▪ ▪

"It is a two-wheeled car. It has nothing to do with a motorcycle" said one motorcyclist. "This is the ultimate touring bike for long-distance travel" cried another. The introduction of the brand-new GL 1000 Gold Wing from Honda had occurred, and in 1974 opinion as to its place was instantly, fiercely, divided.

The Honda flat-four did not merely achieve its goal: it did far better than that. The big machine created a class of its own, with an entire industry providing accessories and ornaments for it.

It is odd to recall that Honda themselves had different goals for the GL 1000. It had been discovered that there was public interest in motorcycles of more than 750cc. Kawasaki underlined the message when the 900cc Z 1 hit the streets. And of course there was the BMW R 90 S. Both machines brought their makers a great deal of prestige. The CB 750 Honda was certainly no longer the absolute top-of-the-market bike in 1972. There appeared to be an interest in even heavier, bigger machines. Honda was apparently reluctant to respond to the impressive 82bhp of the Kawasaki. They did not want a horsepower race. But not being top dogs did worry them; so they proceeded to develop a big bike (as opposed to extracting more power from an existing design). The new Honda was to appeal to the people who were presently buying a BMW or a Kawasaki. The shaft drive of the BMW was appreciated; the performance of the Kawasaki was considered adequate. The first Gold Wing prototype was rather a case of overkill: the

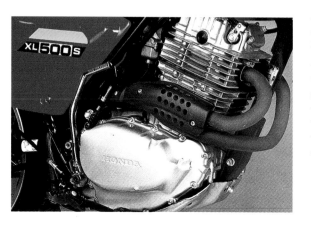

Honda XL 500 engine had plain camshaft bearings as opposed to the roller bearings of the XT. The Honda also featured four valves. On paper it was the winner; in practice the Yamaha usually came out on top.

1973 AOK prototype was a 80bhp 1,500cc flat-six. It was literally built with 'borrowed' frame parts from a BMW. However, the bike was thought to be too long and too heavy. The engineers dropped the six, and went for a flat-four, a 1,000cc unit, giving about 80bhp. All existing ideas about the construction of a motorcycle were set aside. First, the engine was watercooled; only the Suzuki GT 750 had used this technology before. Of course, overhead camshafts was expected in 1974, but drive was by dry toothed belts which was absolutely new at that time. Also new was having the cylinders as part of the crankcase, rather than as separate items.

The tendency of longitudinally mounted engines to turn in the frame was nicely solved on the GL 1000 by having the dynamo rotating in the opposite direction to crankshaft travel, which meant that the counteracting forces eliminated each other. The carburettors and their operation were totally different, too. And the fuel 'tank' was not a fuel tank but merely a cover for the electrics and the air filter. There was even a little glove compartment. A kickstarter lever was under the right panel and could be clipped into the joint on the clutch cover, to start the engine if the battery was flat. (Nobody ever used it, for the electric starter invariably sufficed.) The real fuel tank was under the seat with a camshaft-driven pump delivering fuel to the carburettors. A (rather inaccurate) meter on the top panel monitored contents of the fuel tank. All more than car-like. There were plenty of motorcycles having a double disc brake in the front wheel, but a disc in the rear wheel was new in the early 70s: the Gold Wing had one. The frame was 'different', like the engine. The left lower rail could be removed to dismantle the engine, the frame being built-up from a combination of tubes and profiled sections of sheet metal, all providing adequate stiffness, once assembled. The

Trucks and buses were the only road vehicles to dwarf the 1975 Honda GL 1000 Gold Wing! Entirely new construction features were displayed in this machine.

front engine retainer was massive enough to have come from a car. Nobody really appreciated at the time that this was a complete departure from the normal way of constructing a motorcycle, but later many bikes would be built like the Gold Wing. People were impressed by the size and the weight of the 'Wing in 1974, the year it was first shown. It was 1975 when the first batch was delivered. There were remarkably few teething troubles. The crankshaft of

the first series would occasionally break just behind the clutch; in some cases the engine would keep running even then! (Only the drive would be inoperative, of course.) Synchronisation of the carburettors was very inaccurate:
sometimes just revving too heartily would be enough to call for a resynchronising job! This did not happen when the bike was new, I hasten to say; it only occurred when wear had begun. There could be

an audible clatter from the primary Morse chain (another novelty in the motorcycle world). The shaft drive was also a first for a high-performance bike; a BMW had far less power, and could be serviced easily whereas the joints of a Gold Wing shaft could not be lubricated when servicing the machine. After 35,000 miles the joints generally were pretty well worn out. All later shaft drive motorcycles would benefit from the lessons learnt by Honda with the GL 1000.

Honda promoted the GL 1000 Gold Wing in the same way that they promoted all their other machines. High-speed cruising capability was not emphasised; instead, the GL 1000 was advertised as an all-rounder. But 'racing' was not excluded. Hugh Evans was sponsored by Honda UK in endurance races, riding a GL. The Swiss, Walter Knapp, rode a much-modified Gold Wing in endurance racing too. Many studies were made by Honda of sporting variants of the flat-four, and some of the drawings looked promising. Fortunately, touring versions

were studied too. As early as 1975 there were try-outs with fairings and panniers. The 'all-round' character was best reflected in the first series, the GL 1000 K 1. The engine of this one responded well to high revs; rev it to the red zone and shift gear fast, and you would be surprised how well the K 1 did its stuff. And, all the time, the engine was smooth, absolutely vibration-free. A GL 1000 K 1 would attain more than 125mph in standard trim. A few lessons in marketing were learnt. The days of general marketing of a motorcycle were over. Target groups of people were approached with machines designed to fulfil the wishes of a particular group. BMW fans, for example, would never even look at a Honda. Nor would most Kawasaki riders. Their bikes were not the best handling machines of their time – but in comparison to a Gold Wing, they were pure racers! A GL 1000 was wide and heavy – and the frame was weak. Speed wobbles would occur when the Gold Wing was ridden fast. The rear mudguard was the source of the trouble here, moving and bending and

Large rear mudguard of the first Gold Wing had a tendency to start a steering weave at really high speeds. There was no trouble when the Wing was used as it should be, as a tourer.

Any motorcyclist will recognise the outline of a GL 1000...

causing the rear frame to weave, transmitting movement through the entire motorcycle. High-speed cornering was no fun, either. Scraping sensitive parts over tarmac could cause damage. The result was that sporting riders were soon disappointed in the GL 1000. Much different was the reaction of tourers, with their more relaxed riding style. They never had any problems; simply because they never ran at speeds that could cause problems. Vetter fairings and Krauser pannier sets suited the GL much better than low handlebars and racing fairings.

The Gold Wing had found its place in the market. It was a tourer. Honda rapidly picked up the marketing signals, and adapted their sales campaigns for the big machine. The 1977 GL1000 K2 had few changes over the K 1; modifications mainly came with the 1978 GL 1000 K 3. The kickstarter mechanism with the take-off lever was abolished. The high-shoulder alloy rims were replaced by all-new Comstar wheels, flexible, like wired wheels, but looking like the cast wheels that had become fashionable by 1978. The engine's character was altered to give better pulling power at low revs, at the cost of top speed.

So top speed went down, but nobody noticed. In fact, the bike was being changed to suit the people who were buying it, which made very good sense. Weight went up, but again, nobody was bothered. Tourers are allowed to be heavy. The combined black muffler of the K 1 and K 2 was replaced by chromed, separate mufflers. The black version had had a tendency to rust during an initial test ride! The chromed items were much better.

Production of the Gold Wing was transferred gradually to Honda's American plant. More and more parts were being made in the States. The later GLs would become totally 'American'. Craig Vetter began to sell fairings and sets of panniers like hot cakes, as did Krauser. Then the King-and-Queen seat was born. The shape of this saddle was inspired by a Vincent Rapide dual-seat, so the story goes – and it's possible, I suppose. The resemblance is certainly remarkable. Then there were little lights for the front fork, then covers for the brake discs. Within a very short period, complete catalogues were available, full of dress-up parts for the 'Wing. But this was also a time when burnt-out generators became something of a problem. No account was taken of the fact that so many accessories had to be powered off the generator. The capacity of the unit was increased soon after occurrence of the problems …

The power unit of the K 3 was as reliable as a Honda car's engine. I am talking about a high mileage without major overhauls; and the Gold Wing redefined standards in this area. The GL 1100 came along as successor to the GL 1000 K 3 in 1980: less speed, more tractability was the main characteristic of the bigger engine. And even greater reliability. Very soon there was an 'Interstate' variant. You could go to the dealer if you wanted a full-dress Gold Wing, and didn't fancy doing the job yourself. Fairing and panniers now came as standard equipment. But that did not keep the shops from offering ever more alternative aftermarket parts. The best, the most beautiful, the ugliest, the most useful – or useless – items were listed in the catalogues. The GL 1100 Aspencade arrived in 1982, with the other version, the Interstate, remaining in the lists. Now there was air suspension; an in-built compressor allowed the suspension to be altered, even while riding, for the operating knobs were in the fairing. All this sort of equipment comes in handy for the so-called 'dressers'. A dresser is a person who makes it his hobby to dress up his bike with as many accessories as possible. Competitions are held. It is a diversion well-known to Harley-Davidson owners; and the Gold Wing rapidly became a 'dresser's' bike as well. The horrendous weight of all the accessories can be compensated for by the air suspension.

A change of wheels took place in 1983: the

Comstars were replaced by far more fashionable cast wheels. The frame had grown both in sheer size as well as rigidity. The Aspencade was available with full digital information display, to replace the classic analogue meters. Honda was really very satisfied with the 1100. It was only because of the other manufacturers that the capacity was increased to 1,200cc – to keep Honda ahead. That was in 1984. (Yamaha by then was selling the 1,200cc V-four XVZ 12 Venture; Suzuki had the V-four GV 1400 Cavalcade; and Kawasaki had moved on one step further with the straight-six Z 1300 Voyager.) But it

Where on the Gold Wing you would expect the fuel tank to be, there was the expansion tank for the cooling system. On the other side, the electrics were concentrated.

Each bank of cylinders (integrated in the crankcase) is served by one camshaft. Operation of the four constant-vacuum carburettors is inaccurate.

Camshafts were operated by toothed belts, at the time – another novelty in motorcycle construction.

High-shoulder alloy rims were standard, as was the double disc; with the disc in the rear wheel the Gold Wing became the first all-disc-brake motorcycle.

Counter-rotating clutch eliminated the 'twisting effect' (as in a BMW Boxer). Hy-vo chains were responsible for the smooth running of the flat-four engine.

The 1978 GL 1000 K 3 had Comstar wheels and the gauges in the console on the 'tank'. It was the last of the 1000s. Power had come down, touring ability was improved.

Apparently, the Kawasaki Z 1's prestige hit a raw nerve at Honda. After a period of comparative rest, plans to bring out successors to the very successful four-cylinders initiated by the CB 750 had to be put in train. The RCB endurance racer led to the Bol d'Or models, as a natural next step. The second half of the 1970s had already brought the world the Yamaha XS 1100 and the Suzuki GS 1000; not to forget the range of 1000cc Kawasakis. The development engineers were granted a free hand.

What they did was spot on! They were inspired by Honda's famous six-cylinder racer of the sixties, the RC 164. That machine was considered the most exciting racer of all time. Only Honda could turn out a modern replica of that superb six. The name of the prototype was CB X. CB stood for sports tourer; the X for 1000, or 1100. Late in 1978 the 1047cc CB X was for sale everywhere. The six-cylinder masterpiece was a slap in the face for Yamaha with their XS 1100, and Suzuki's GS 1000. The press loved the CB X; they could hardly believe that such beauty was for sale over the counter. Kawasaki's Z 1000, too, was outclassed.

The six-cylinder CB X was a technical marvel of the first degree. Twenty-four valves had to be checked when servicing the bike; four hollow camshafts, coupled in pairs by special couplers, were driven by

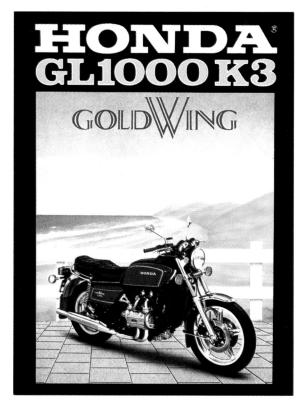

a toothed chain. The 'exhausts' were driven from the crankshaft, and a second Morse chain had the exhaust cams power the intake cams. The racer had a cam gear train; that expensive solution was not adopted for the CB X (later it would appear in the VF 1000 R). Apart from the camshaft drive, the whole CB X was a sort of enlarged copy of, and a tribute to, the racer. The engine was a stressed member of the frame, taking the place of normal lower rails.

The aircooled powerplant was a typical short-stroke engine – which implies use of relatively large pistons. When six pistons are arranged alongside each other, special measures have to be taken to keep engine width within limits. The primary Morse

Kawasaki Z 1300 is a big motorcycle. The engine alone weighs 128kg and does not contribute to the strength of the cycle parts. The frame, consequently, has to be heavy and strong.

chain in the middle of the crankshaft drove an auxiliary shaft, with ignition and generator powered from the auxiliary shaft. All these items were situated behind the wide cylinder block with the result that the engine was less than an inch wider than the length of the crankshaft. Such a construction was to be commonplace 10 years on. A CB X engine was narrower than a CB 750's, measured over the cases. The drive to keep weight down was very evident in little things, such as hollow bolts and thin castings. A 1047cc CB X engine weighs less than a CB 750 powerplant, the outcome being that the total weight of the motorcycle was relatively low too, at 260kg. A real 'first' was that the Honda CB X was the first bike to exceed the magic frontier of 100bhp, albeit by a mere 5bhp.

In spite of the relatively large size of the bike (especially in comparison to more modern machinery), the CB X was a pure sports bike. It was, therefore, a welcome addition in the Honda range to

Dynamo of the CB X was situated behind the cylinders, contributing to the slim lines of the straight six. Engine width, measured over the crankcases, is less than that of a CB 750.

the touring Gold Wing. The big engine was supposed to run at 10,000rpm, and would easily exceed that on the road. The CB X was in its element at high revs; below 3,000rpm nobody was at home! Unfortunately, the sound of the exhaust was, well, very modest. However, the music that more open, aftermarket system could produce on a CB X was really far out – an echo of the racer: hair-raising! There were a few items of the CBX that were rather conventional. The front fork, for instance, was somewhat undersized. If the brakes were made to work hard, the forks bent. Literally. And those brakes were not really all that powerful ...The rear suspension was by twin dampers. They were the first generation of really good shock absorbers to come from Japan. The fact that there were two of them made the rear suspension conventional. Fast riding through long open turns was thrilling – but not in the way that the makers, presumably, planned. All this should not suggest that a fast ride along country

Front wheels: light and elegant Comstar of the CB X versus the heavy, strong cast wheel of the Big Zed. The same might be said of the brakes and front forks of the two machines.

(below left) Where the rider of a CB X sits the bike is slim and well proportioned, like a 'normal' sports bike.

lanes on a CB X was not, in the main, a joy. A later version of the original six, the CB X B Pro-Link, is not much appreciated nowadays. Yet it had really all the answers to the objections raised against the early CB X. The 1983 Pro-Link had a sophisticated rear suspension with one damper operated by a link system that provided progressive operation. The much thicker fork legs carried double-piston brake calipers biting on ventilated discs. Handling was very good. The fairing that came with the Pro-Link was well designed, allowing a rider comfortable 100mph cruising. It is true, however, that the engine was detuned a trifle. This, together with the added weight, moved the bike into sports-tourer territory. Truth is, a Pro-Link is anonymous, whereas a flamboyant old model CB X attracts the eye.

KAWASAKI Z 1300

Like the CB X, the Z 1300 is a six-cylinder motorcycle. This is about all they have in common. The (original) CB X Z or CB X A was a totally sporty machine and was, essentially, logically constructed. The Kawasaki Z 1300 was, and is, a pile of contradictions. The presentation of the 120bhp monster caused even more commotion than the CB X. The watercooled Z 1300 has only two valves per cylinder and normal double camshafts. The press wondered openly whether the average motorcyclist would be able to control so much power. It was this motorcycle, the Z 1300, that caused the Germans to insist that no motorcycles producing more than 100bhp should be imported. The Z 1300

is a long-stroke engine. You'd expect it to have a heavy crankshaft, which would imply lots of power at low rpm. But the Kawasaki confounded all expectations. Its ultra-light crankshaft made high revs possible, and there was a lot of low-end power. If you took off with no feeling for the clutch the engine would stall, because of that light crank; yet the Zed could be ridden at 1,500rpm in top gear! And if you are lazy, forget abut gear-shifting: the Kawa will *go*. From 6,000rpm, the acceleration will increase until it hits

Wide, high seat of the Kawasaki Z 1300 renders manhandling the machine difficult, but also means that a trip of 500 miles can be made in comfort.

a wall at 8,750rpm, when the ignition cries halt. Top speed is higher than that of a CB X. A Honda will beat a Kawa on the dragstrip, however. In fact a CB X beats most things on a dragstrip!

A Kawasaki Z 1300 is geared to do exactly 151mph at 8,750rpm. At that speed, the huge forks of the Z 1300 are solid as rock. There's never the slightest weave. The brakes have a lot of work to do stopping more than 320kg; but they are up to their job. Gear-changing can be fast and sharp. Yet there is shaft drive to the massive rear wheel. A CB X with its chain, and link system for the gear pedal, is beaten in this area. But who would call a bike that is larger, in overall size, than a Honda Gold Wing a sports bike? It is not a real tourer, either. A Z 1300 sounds like a six-cylinder roadgoing MV Agusta would have

sounded, if such a beast had existed.

A Zed loses revs very rapidly, thanks to that light crankshaft. It encourages much gear-shifting, and speeding. You may be tempted to conclude that the Z 1300 is perfect. It is not. In spite of the factory claiming to have covered thousands of miles in the deserts while testing prototypes, the bike overheats. There is simply not enough cooling capacity in the watercooled system; 3.5 pints is too little. In a traffic jam the rider is roasted by the engine! And soon it will start running on five, then four, then three cylinders. And finally on none: vapour lock in those specially designed Mikuni carburettors. Then you can do nothing but wait for the bike to cool down. In any case, the starter motor will have become so hot that it has no power left to crank the engine.

The Honda CB X is a sporting machine that handles like a 750 of the same age. It has astonishing ground clearance and in general is very user-friendly; anybody can ride it.

Another facet of the big Kwacker is the 'two-week cold start'. It will either start at the first revolution of the crank – or not at all. (The latter more often, of course.) The standard cure is to take the carburettor plugs out; let petrol escape for a while, and put the plugs in again. Then full choke and a little twist of the throttle. If it does not start, do the whole thing again. Don't be tempted to get the starter motor cranking the engine for long; that will not help; you will only flatten the battery. The engine starts immediately, or not at all! This mainly happens if you ride only occasionally. Once it runs, you can confidently stop the engine; the lightest touch of the button will be effective next time round. If the Kawa is used daily, it always starts immediately. But after 14 days …

The same subject, starting, as experienced with the CB X… Press the button on the right. Use the handlebar-mounted choke. When the engine catches, gently close the choke lever until the engine ticks over nicely. When the engine is warm, don't use the choke. A little different from the Kawasaki rigmarole …

There's one item on a Z 1300 that's a little weak, on the mechanical side. The tensioner of the Morse cam chain is undersized. It is always due for replacement after 10,000 miles. An easy job; but still …And the first series suffered from a real teething trouble, when too little oil was used in the wet sump: 4.6 litres was a lot, but not enough. The intake of the oil-pump was positioned too high, and of course air bubbles are not a good lubricant. When collecting the modification kit at the importers, I've seen a few intriguing conrods that had peeped outside the crankcase, through holes that were not planned! Always number 1 and number 6. I managed to pull the clutch and shut the throttle before that happened with me; I'd heard trouble coming at 120mph. I even made it to home – another 160 miles, at 2,000rpm.

With this trouble sorted out in 1980, on the A 2, the bike has become mechanically very reliable. Now there are 6.2 litres of oil in the pan, which helps cooling a little, too. And, of course, the oil system was altered drastically to go with the increase of oil capacity. Now a regularly used Z 1300 can notch up 100,000 miles without overhaul, although it's fair to say the bike uses oil. This remained a Kawasaki characteristic for many years, rather more so with the Z 1300 since piston speed can reach more than 23 metres per second, at 8,000rpm, where the generally accepted safe limit is 19 metres/second.

It's a long stroke, remember? A CB X hardly exceeds 15 metres/second.

A lot of extreme statements have been made about the stupid/adorable (choose your adjective!) Z 1300. You will have guessed that this is one love it or hate it machine. You hate it if you have to start it after some time of non-use. You immediately know again why you bought it when you speed up the lane towards the highway …

If you adapt yourself properly to the Z 1300 you can feel in heaven when riding the beast. If you don't, you are very likely to get into trouble. The Kawasaki does not forgive any mistakes.

Z 1300: seven main bearings, six big-ends and many transmission parts mean expensive engine overhauls. The first series did break down, but after modifications to the oil system there were no problems.

Behind the side cover of the Z 1300 is an extra safety device. The ignition key can immobilize the bike; the corner of the side cover pivots to unveil the extra switch.

■ ■ Choose ■ ■

The Z 1300 begs comparison with a truck, while a CB X is a nicely proportioned sportsbike. A Kawa is tough, like a bulldog. It may become beautiful if you stare at it for a long time; but probably not. A Honda is a beauty from whatever angle you look at it. You will automatically stare a long time at the RC 164 replica. A CB X makes a lot of mechanical noise, especially when stationary. A Z 1300 is mechanically almost completely silent, although there are seven chains in the engine. The long stroke 'dances' when stationary, because of that light crank. A CB X crank is heavier than that of a Z 1300, when of course you would expect the opposite. A Honda does not make much of a special sound in standard trim, but when a six-into-one exhaust is added, the story changes. The 'bite' of the Zed makes you ride it as if it was a CB X, when you will learn that the heavy bike uses far less petrol than a 105bhp CB X.

A CB X can be ridden by anyone. Immediately, one is at home on a Honda. It handles and feels like a normal motorcycle, while a Z 1300 takes quite a while to get used to. For example, shutting the throttle in a turn will not elicit the best sort of behaviour from a Z 1300. In severe cases, the rear wheel will step out. Most people, I'm convinced, never get used to a Z 1300, but the owner that can adapt to it will be able to do more with a Z 1300 than with a CB X. A nice comparison occurs when the front tyre is low on pressure. A CB X can be ridden with an almost flat front tyre, whereas a Kawasaki is almost uncontrollable when pressure is a few lb/in down.

Approximately 14 000 Z 1300s are believed to have been made. Commercially, the Kawa was a failure, while the Honda was a success. Yet the prestige of the Kawasaki exceeds that of the Honda six. Both are, undeniably, classics and it is unlikely that such spectacular six-cylinder motorcycles will be built again. In fact, Kawasaki made a statement in this direction… Before long both the sixes will be given the classic treatment that the Vincent Black Shadow is accorded today. And rightly so.

Now which one would I choose, having compared them so thoroughly? Both have a lot of pros and cons. I'd liken a fight between the sixes to a boxing match. The CB X fights beautifully, with a lot of fast legwork, yet the Z 1300 wins by points in the end. I hate the Zed when I have to start it, for I know it takes a lot of time. The thrill of the sound while accelerating on the motorway makes up for that. Then again, I would not want to miss the superb tribute to the RC 164 racer that CB X is; fortunately, I don't have to choose…

Twenty-four CB X valves take a lot of work to check or adjust; and so does synchronising the six carburettors. The clutch is more than up to its task.

Air-cooling versus watercooling: how the sixes differ.
Both are very desirable machines.

GL 500 Silver Wing: a sort of CX 500 in Gold Wing
guise. Like its big brother it became popular, but it did
not project the same sort of charisma as the flat-four.

THE EIGHTIES
THE MARKET WIDENS

In the 1970s we could connect a certain range of motorcycles to a certain make. As in: four-cylinders with Honda; wild two-stroke triples with Kawasaki; sophisticated two-stroke triples – typically Suzuki; four-stroke twins – Yamaha. This was no longer possible halfway through the 1980s. And by 1990 almost every kind of motorcycle concept one can think of was in existence, turned out by all four makers! 'Typical Suzuki' or 'typical Yamaha' hardly exist in the 90s. What does exist are model ranges that are successful or failures. The lines of development became obscure during the eighties. Public and press complained about the continuous stream of new models. General standards of quality were so high that models with real faults were rare indeed. Model ranges sometimes last only a year or two. If a particular model is here to stay, it nonetheless changes every year! Often, the changes are merely cosmetic. Rapid devaluation of your newly acquired motorcycle is the inevitable result. In the first half of the eighties a depression in the world economy had – of course – an effect on motorcycling too. The 'boom' slowed, only to resume around 1987-88, when more and more people who would never have considered riding a motorcycle bought a bike and found themselves enjoying a new freedom. Directors, lawyers, doctors – all were recruits to motorcycling! And often on a big custom bike. After all, he or she could afford it. Bikes became more luxurious, and expensive, with each passing year. Secondhand bikes sold for more than they had cost five or six years earlier, when new. Europeans bought almost all the surplus from the USA. Television began to pay some limited attention to the motorcycle, with screen advertisements for household goods, clothes and the like, featuring bikes. By the end of the eighties riding a motorcycle had become fashionable.

This CX 500 Sports can be seen as a restyled and improved CX 500. After discontinuation of the model some time elapsed before Honda created a worthy successor.

A totally new model was the 1978 Honda CX 500 that came together with the CB X and was somewhat overshadowed by the six. It had a pushrod four-valve engine that could spin at 10,000 rpm.

CX engine had cylinders integrated in the castings of the crankcases, like the Gold Wing. The crankshaft, however, was mounted in a sort of subframe, very unlike the GL 1000.

The machines divided by type rather than by make. Example: the only thing the following bikes have in common is the name of their maker – XR 600, VT 600, GL 1500, CB 125, NSR 400, CBR 1000. All Hondas. But they could be different makes if compared one to another. The same could be said for Suzuki or Yamaha or Kawasaki.

The 1978 CB 750 Bol d'Or was successor to the legendary CB 750. 'Eurostyle' model did not have the impact of the CB X, but 900cc version performed almost as well as the six-cylinder CB X.

After the GL 1000 K 3 the Gold Wing was enlarged by 100cc and became this 1981 GL 1100. It was a better tourer than the already 'perfect' older model. Tractability improved; top speed dropped.

Trouble for Honda. This VF 750 C (and its stablemates, the F and the S) had problems with camshaft lubrication. It took years before these were sorted out, in the second generation of vee-fours.

There was a growing interest in classic bikes. The classic Japanese motorcycle was 'discovered'. A collector who had a Triumph Bonneville and a Norton Commando began to show interest in a Suzuki T 500 or a Honda Black Bomber. Bikes of the seventies are – in many cases – still very viable in modern traffic. A Suzuki GT 750, a Honda CB 750, a Kawasaki 900, a Yamaha XS 650 … all can still do what is required on the road even in the nineties. And then yet another type of bike was discovered or, rather, invented: the retro bike. A retro is a more or less modern machine that looks like an old one, usually having something of a 70s look.

THE NON-JAPANESE COMEBACK

A very unexpected phenomenon of the eighties was the revival among the European manufacturers; as well as Harley-Davidson of the USA. Harley-Davidson was not able to produce enough Evolution engines to meet demand for their bikes. The Evo was not, objectively, a bad machine; and of course Harley men just loved them. The Japanese seemed doomed never to make an effective copy of the true heart of a Harley. In Europe, Ducati did not disintegrate when Cagiva took over; indeed now Ducati flourishes as never before. In the past Ducati always suffered from a cash shortage. Now Cagiva provides the funds for developing new models, and there's no crisis in the accounts to bedevil the engineers. I'd say Ducatis are not, yet, on a par with the Japanese in the quality department. The shortfall is not as great as in the seventies, when the question was not if, but when,

your Ducati would break down! So – all thanks to Cagiva.

Moto Guzzi are struggling, but manage to survive with the distinctive V-twins. The Daytona 1000, the Dr. John Special, shows the way they will go, I hope. A California with a Dr. John engine, perhaps? There seems to blow a fresh new wind in Mandello del Lario, Italy. Nowadays, even Laverda seems to have risen from the ashes, with the new 650 Sport. Later models (now there is a watercooled 750) certainly look very promising. BMW has two ranges of bikes that have loyal followers. The new generation Boxer flat-twins will have followers till death do them part. The in-line K series sell well. Even MZ, now MuZ, may survive; the Skorpion may be an augury for the former East German make. What John Bloor has done with his Triumph motorcycles is unbelievable. Against the stream, he managed to establish a modern line of three- and four-cylinder motorcycles, setting up a hyper-modern way of producing them. The triples especially have established a respectable place in the market. Their quality? As good as that of the Kawasakis he tended to follow. Now he has abandoned the Kawasaki origin, and the machines are even more desirable. Norton is a different story. Perhaps Bloor may manage something with that famous name? We'll have to wait, and see. The Koreans have started an offensive, showing their first developments in the western world. Not yet entirely to Japanese standards; but not far off … Hyundai, Kia, Daewoo and more car makers from Korea are carving a piece of the action in the car world for themselves. Will Korean motorcycles be next? All this story may sound like history in reverse. Who is to tell? The Japanese are beginning to have problems keeping costs under control – bikes made in Japan are becoming expensive. Novel ideas, mainly originating in Europe, still have a chance, and may become the basis of future developments. The Bimota Mantra and the Aprilia Moto 6.5 are just two examples...

HONDA

Honda entered the eighties with the 1978 'Euroline'. The CB 750 KZ and Bol d'Or models were about the place, in different shapes. Classic lines, sporty lines; with or without fairings. The frame with the detachable rail, introduced on the Gold Wing, was more modern than the old CB 750 setup. It should have made dismantling the bike easier but didn't. The most interesting part was the engine, a

developed version of the 1970s RCB endurance racer. There were two overhead camshafts operating four valves per cylinder by a rather special drive. The exhaust cam was driven by a Morse chain with a second toothed chain from the exhaust driving the inlet. The engines were nicely constructed, and far more civilised than the sohc CB 750s they replaced. Styling was considered very important in the late seventies and early eighties, and these bikes looked really 'modern'. Suspension had benefited from the progress of technology, and rider comfort was good. But there was a downside too. The newly designed frame was responsible for frequent speed wobbles. The old CB 750 had been better at high speed. And the new engine tended to wear more rapidly than the old one. But, still, sales were good.

The CB X, that topped the model range, has been described already. The last Pro-Link version was sold in 1984, and nothing having the charisma of

that potent six-cylinder succeeded it.

Next to the fours, Honda had built up a following for their twin-cylinder line that can be traced back to the CB 72 of 1960. Throughout the seventies a whole range of rather nondescript twins had appeared. In 1978 the CB 250 and 400 T and 400 N were born. The CB 400 N achieved some popularity, even to the extent of siring a special race category. In the custom department, there was the CM 400 T variant. This little bike was popular in riding schools and among learner motorcyclists. Women, also, liked the easy-to-handle machine. The three-valve sohc engine was lively and performed well. However, it was not particularly long-lived: by 20,000 miles it was usually worn out. The 400 was followed by the 450 and a space-frame CB 450 S. Bread-and-butter bikes. One step up in capacity, there was the last of the sohc fours, the CB 650 in, again, various shapes: a custom, a would-be classic

Honda was quite satisfied with the 1100, but to stay ahead of the pack the factory developed the Gold Wing into the GL 1200 in 1982. The formula worked, for the machine remained the most successful tourer.

The 1983 CBX 750 in-line four served as a sort of back-up for vee-four machines. Honda was suffering reliability troubles instead of being clearly in the lead.

and an all-rounder. But they were not very distinctive – were not as good as the sohc fours from the seventies.

In 1978 another, rather more interesting, model began life. The CX 500 was, like the Gold Wing, a departure from normal practice. Some Gold Wing-like features were to be found on the CX 500, such as integrated cylinders, and the counter-rotating clutch, to cope with reaction forces. The V-twin pushrod engine had the cylinder heads turned out, to enable the carburettors to be mounted closer to the centre of the frame, and away from the knees of the rider. The technical achievements to be seen in the CX were impressive but, still, there were troubles. The camchain tensioner wasn't strong enough, for one thing. But it's fair to say that once this snag had been overcome, the bike went on to build up a reputation for durability. Many courier companies used it as workhorse. The bike's looks, as well as its specification, were a departure from normal practice. Many people used to call it a slug! In 1981, a custom version was introduced, together with the Turbo. The CX 500 C model (for custom) was a very popular machine.

For Gold Wing lovers short of money or who couldn't handle such a big lump, there was the GL 500 Silver Wing – a CX 500 in Gold Wing guise. The CX models grew to 650cc in the second phase of their life, to become ever more popular. Rightly so, for these shaft-drive middle-class machines were very nice to ride. They did everything right. When Honda dropped them in 1986, they were soon to regret doing so. The VT 500 E was not a worthy successor. After a while, the NVT 650 Revere took over the role. Secondhand CX 500s and 650s remain

Happier times arrived for Honda with this model, the 1983 VT 500 C. It was to be followed by many more Shadows, ranging from 500 to 1100cc.

high priced. Ten years on, they may even turn out to be classics – who knows!

In the commuter department, there were CB and CD 125 and 200 twins, plus numerous C 50, 70 and 90 variants. Descendants of the original 1958 C 100 Super Cub will probably still be on sale, somewhere in the world, in 2098! The CB 250 RS was tried out on the commuter market. A nice machine, and a street version of the off-road XL 250, the RS did not meet expectations. The FT 500 Ascot, a derivative of the XL 500, was a failed attempt to make a 500cc single street bike; for one thing, its dirt-track racer looks were not appreciated. Another street version of an off-roader, the XL-based XBR 500, was a disappointment. It was such a pleasant bike too! A later version, the GB 500, was even nicer.

The XL off-road series was a success, however. An XL 500 was more sophisticated than a Yamaha XT 500, although the Yamaha sold better. The two machines dominated this sector of the motorcycle market. The other two makers were far behind. The XR 500, later 600, enduro derivative became the standard in the (small) roadgoing competition bike market.

Among sports bikes and all-rounders, Honda tried new ideas. The days of the traditional four-cylinder in-line motorcycle seemed to be numbered. Honda had suffered setbacks in this field, because the Bol d'Ors were not regarded as 'mainstream' models. Every manufacturer sold bikes that could be classified as examples of the UJM (universal Japanese

SEHEN SIE'S '84 GANZ GELASSEN.
HONDA CHOPPER.

motorcycle). The Kawasaki GPz and the Suzuki GXS models were the successful ones, and Honda felt a need to maintain face, and so created the CB 1100 R, a beauty of a bike that really handled well and had a decent performance. The problem was that it was extremely expensive. And it was only built in small numbers. Honda concluded that V-fours might be the answer. For those who still wanted an in-line four, the Bol d'Or was succeeded by the CBX 400, 550, 650 and 750 models. All rather anonymous. They handled well enough, in fact they were good bikes, but they failed to attract any real attention. More plastic was introduced, and the graphics were designed to give the bike a 'one-piece' look. The inboard disc of the CBX 550 had the looks of a drum brake, which was very clever, though it was a complicated matter to get either of the wheels out.

The vee-fours, however, were the bikes that Honda expected to score with. There was a sports version, the VF 750 F. The custom was called the VF 750 C and there was a VF 750 S, which had shaft drive, but was still a rather sporty bike. These were the backbone of the range. Soon there were 400, 500 and 1,000cc sizes of V-fours in custom, all-rounder and sports variations. Only a 'tourer' was missing in the range. The Gold Wing performed so well that it just went on and on. The VFs were nice bikes to ride, all of them. They were fast, and fun to take into long, open-road bends. The small front wheel, then fashionable, made the steering quick, some would even say nervous. Top speed of the VF 750 S was around 125mph and the F was even faster. Even a VF 500 F would reach 125mph. The brakes were good; but not excellent.

There was a major problem with the V-four range. The oil took too long to reach the camshafts when the bike was started. Capacity of the oil-pump was too low, in any case, and the camchain tensioners were of very poor quality. Many V-fours spent a lot of time in the workshop, even within the warranty period. Camshafts that ran dry, or at least wore rapidly, and skipping camchains caused a lot of disasters. It was a long time before Honda took any action, and it all left many customers very unhappy. A lot of blame was heaped on the owners – taking off too fast on a cold engine, and so on – and with some justice. However it was basically Honda's fault. The model range continued, and it was fortunate that the CBX bikes were OK. The snags of the Vee engines were cured, eventually. The 1984 VF 1000 R, taking the place of the CB 1100 R, showed the

way to a solution. This exclusive machine had cam gear trains instead of chains, with their wretched tensioners (I replaced a few of them!). The gear-driven cams were, of course, 1960s racing technology; but they did the trick. The VF 1000 R was the only bike to benefit at first. Like the CB 1100 R, it was only built in small numbers, and it was very expensive. But such a superior machine to ride! I've never felt so confident with 160mph on the speedo in a long turn. To illustrate their strategy of trying to fill any gap in the model programme, Honda even built a two-stroke. The NSR 400 was a remarkable three-cylinder, one cylinder up and two flat. It was meant to be an answer to Suzuki's RG 500 square four and the Yamaha RD 500 LC, also a four. But the NSR 400 was no match for the competition. Giving away 100cc was too much. (The Japanese domestic market was another story, for there the 400cc class was big business.)

HONDA IN THE SECOND HALF OF THE EIGHTIES

Something needed to be done: Honda was worried. They had been overtaken by their rivals in many ways. The V-fours suffered from a public perception of unreliability; the little parallel twins were being strongly challenged by the other manufacturers; the in-line fours were overshadowed by the Suzuki GSX and the Kawasaki GPZ ranges. The GPZ 900 R, especially, showed up the blandness of the Honda fours. Things would only get worse when the Yamaha FZ and the Suzuki GSX R came out. Custom

XR 600 R was Honda's ace in the off-road and enduro department. It became the bike to beat in this sector.

VF 1000 R showed the way to better vee-fours for Honda. This expensive 1984 successor to the CB 1100 R of 1981 had the cam troubles sorted out. Later VFRs benefitted from the machine.

bikes were another grey area for Honda. The VT 500 C had yet to become successful. Only the Gold Wing was still in the lead, in the touring world. The off-roaders were doing well, however, with XL and XR models preferred by the majority of interested riders. Eventually Honda managed to overtake Yamaha, market leader for many years. The electric-start XL 600 LM, with its huge tank, was a success; the VT

600-based Transalp ditto. It was seen as a roadgoing bike with the suspension of an off-roader. If a Transalp now is considered too tame, there is the Africa Twin, more or less a Transalp in battledress. The answer to Honda's misfortunes in the in-line four field came in 1986. Interest in this particular configuration had not vanished, so it appeared. The CBR 600 and CBR 1000 were superb machines, the

600 becoming the yardstick of success in the 600 cc sports bike category. Initially, only Kawasaki had an answer with the GPZ 600 R. The Honda was the winner, however. The styling of the CBR series was innovative; the Ducati Paso had been first with the idea of an all-enclosed bike, but Honda designed and manufactured their fairing so well that it became the new standard. Critics have called it a plastic bike, but they were wrong; the CBRs were good, very good. A sigh of relief might have been heard in the offices of Honda importers worldwide: "Finally, an engine with no complications". I have said that the CBR 1000 was a 'less sporty' model, and that shows the rising standards of the late eighties. A CBR 1000 would easily reach 160mph. The handling was impeccable; braking too.

In an effort to give an answer to the hyper sport Yamaha FZ 750 and Suzuki GSX R 750, Honda introduced the RC 30, also known as the VFR 750 R. This bike was a jewel, with its single-side rear-wheel suspension; and the distinctive sound of the gear-driven cams in the V-four engine was a joy. The beautiful frame was covered by plastic work in the battle colours of HRC (Honda Racing Corporation). The problem was that it cost one and a half times the price of its competitors; and it was not one and a half times as good. Or much faster.

The custom market was another segment in which Honda regained terrain. The V-four customs developed into the VF Magnas and became popular, once the cam problem had been overcome. Customs are ridden more gently so lubrication is generally less critical than in a sports bike. After 1987, the Magnas were very good.

The V-twin Shadow range that started with the VT 500 developed into a success, with a proliferation of models in various sizes: 500, 600, 700, 750, 800 and 1100. The competition from Yamaha's XV Viragos, Kawasaki Vulcans and Suzuki Intruders was fierce, but Honda remained on its feet, even if it was not a clear winner. If there was a winner, it was probably Harley-Davidson. Almost all the V-twin customs try so hard to be a Harley. Technically, of course, the Japanese are superior, but what matters in a custom bike is the 'feeling' it gives the rider. And here Harley, undeniably, is the winner.

After 1987, the marketing strategy changed. The much-criticised flood of new models (many not mentioned in these pages) ebbed. More 'focussed' models were marketed. One result was that the rate of depreciation of secondhand bikes slowed. By the end of the 1980s, Honda had overcome the dip in

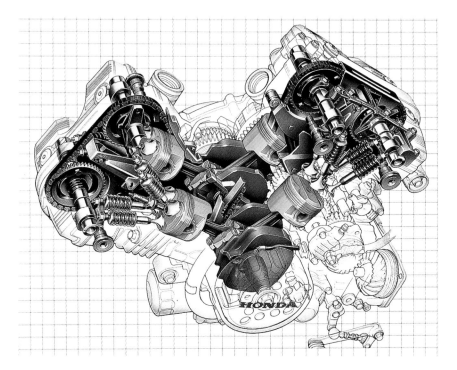

First and second generation of Honda vee-fours. Cam chains of the early engines were replaced by the gear trains of the VFRs. Also improved was the lubrication.

sales suffered in the first half of the decade. The NVT 650 Revere, or Hawk in the USA, successor to the CX 650, began to find a place in the market. A V-twin, the cylinders arranged longitudinally, was a very good all-round machine, even better probably than the good old CX. It was down to the Revere to take over from the CX 650 in the rôle of dependable middleweight. The vee-fours, that had given so many problems, moved into a new, third generation. The 1987 VFR 750 became a very, very good all-round motorcycle, with all problems overcome. Together with the CBR variants, the VFR models moved into the nineties. The ageing Gold Wing begat a successor, another 'Wing, but with more of everything: the 1500cc flat-six has more capacity than the earlier bikes, more weight, more tractability.

A sigh of relief from Honda dealers greeted the 1987 CBR 600, which made clear that the in-line four layout had plenty of life left. It was conventional, but very good. The CBR 600 started the now popular 600cc sports bike class.

With the CBR range for sporting riders, the second generation of vee-fours, the VFRs, developed into well loved sports-tourers. This is the VFR 750 of 1987.

(right) On the basis of the custom VT models, this all-round NVT 650 Revere vee-twin was developed as successor to the successful CX 500 and 650. The model was far better than its public reception might have suggested.

It is more expensive, too. Success! Exactly 25 years after the 1500cc prototype AOK six, the ultimate touring bike had been created. Thought to be impossible in 1973, the flat-six has shown it can be a commercial success. The retro-bike, started by Kawasaki, has an effective Honda representative in the form of the CB 1000 'Big One', a 'naked' CBR 1000 given the looks of the now classic CB 1100 R. The modern watercooled engine and the lines of the R made a good combination. But Honda got the price wrong, so it was not a big seller. A Kawasaki Zephyr was cheaper, and therefore sold better. One other future classic was born at the end of the decade. The ST 1100 Pan-European was developed in Germany. Honda's engineers had gone to the home of their chief competitor in the field, BMW. They wanted to develop their BMW K 100 RT challenger in the 'right' environment. The ST 1100 became a huge success in the nineties. It was (and still is), simply, a superb machine.

KAWASAKI IN THE EIGHTIES

The smallest of the Big Four had a relatively limited programme of models at the beginning of the 1980s. All the models were four-strokes; the era of the two-stroke was finally over. The entire Kawasaki range consisted of twins and fours, with poppet valves. There were the Z 250 and Z 400 twins, to begin with, which were soon followed by LTD custom variants. They were not very highly regarded; the comparable Hondas were doing rather better, and it seemed that customs didn't really fit the 'Kawasaki' image. Exception to the rules was the Z 200 single, a commuter combining a sporty flavour with down-to-earth usage. It was not really that sporty, or even very good, but it sold quite well. The Z 400 J and 500 fours were good machines but lacked charisma; however, thanks to the fact that the other manufacturers had no fours in these capacity classes, the Zs managed to sell. But as Yamaha and Suzuki brought out fours, the Kawas vanished into obscurity.

A sports image was something that was linked to Kawasaki – thanks to those two-stroke triples of the seventies. It was the big in-line four-cylinders that put Kawasaki on the map in later years. The various forms in which the Z 1000 went on sale made Kawasaki the major seller in this area: the Z 1 R sports bike, the Z 1000 ST shaft drive, the Z 1000 J, the Z 1000 Mk2 – all were available in 1981. From 1982, a new range was added that

immediately caught the attention of the motorcycle community. The GPz line consisted of 550, 750 and 1100 variants. Their distinctive red and black colouring, performance, and the ruggedness of the engines made for success. The Z 650 was really a bike of the 1970s, but continued to be sold in the eighties. All these models were in fact based on the illustrious Z 1 of 1972. The aircooled, two-valves-per-cylinder engines were not as modern as the Hondas and Suzukis, but responded well to tuning, leading to bikes with that elusive quality of 'character'. Their raw power, allied to the aggressive styling of the GPz range, made them best-sellers. More variants appeared, some mildly styled, like the Z 550 and 750 GT – both unburstable workhorses. Their bland looks kept them out of the spotlight, yet they were to remain available throughout the eighties.

The more radically styled Z 750 and 1000 R models became popular, topped by the Eddie Lawson Replicas fashioned after the bike Lawson rode in the US Superbike races. During the nineties, this model became increasingly sought after and developed classic status. During the eighties, the GPz range played first violin. Another eye catcher, the Z 1300, stayed in the line-up until 1986, being equipped, from '84, with fuel injection. Remember what we said about starting the bike? Large sales were never achieved for the six, the model serving to prove a point. Fuel injection was also used on the GPz 1100. There had been experimental Z 1000s fitted with this replacement for carburettors, but the GPz 1100 was seen as the bike to feature this novelty in motorcycling. The Kawasaki fours moved to the top

One of the first production motorcycles with fuel injection was the 1978 Kawasaki Z 1000 Injection. It was based on the Z 1000, which was evolved from the famous Z 1.

The legendary Z1000 is "born again" with more power, more style more refinement – and better than ever with a shaft drive system.

You can never get too much of a good thing. Kawasaki's good old Z1 in 1972 blew the competition into the weeds with its amazing blend of high performance and reliability. It set a whole new standard for superbikes. Every year Kawasaki worked to improve it in many subtle ways. A natural process of engineering evolution. And the Big Z always got

better, never older. This year it's been "born again" with so many new features you should think of it as a brand new machine—with a fabulous history.
Introducing the Z1000ST: an old friend with a new shaft drive. Just about the only thing you'll recognize about the Z1000ST which you may remember from its previous lives, is the the remarkable engine. This

tried and true powerhouse—probably the winningest stock engine in motorcycle history in production races around the world—is stronger than ever. It delivers more power with less stress. Greater reliability with lower maintenance. The new Z1000ST with shaft drive is the big bike you know you can live with for the long haul. You can take it on trust.

Seventies Z 1000 was developed into the shaft-drive Z 1000 ST. This smaller stablemate of the Z 1300 was joined by many successful (bigger and smaller), mostly chain-drive, brothers in the eighties.

Fuel-injected GPz 1100 of 1983 was the last of the models that can be traced back to the old Z 1. It was very, very successful in spite of the dated origin of the engine.

of the pile in the early eighties. Only the Suzuki GSXs were really competitive.

The off-road sector was difficult for Kawasaki. The little two-strokes made no impression, nor did the KL 250 four-stroke. The custom market was another field in which Kawasaki did not seem at ease, even though the company had been first in this one, with the 1976 Z 900 LTD. A sporty four-cylinder was just not the right engine for a custom; a big twin, be it a parallel or a V-twin, was considered to be far more suitable. Kawasaki missed the boat they had launched themselves. The Z 750 and the 1100 Spectre were unsuccessful, although they were good bikes.

When the Turbo race started in 1981, Kawasaki came out as second-best (although some say the turbo Kawa won the race). An important model for Kawasaki arrived on the scene in 1983, again in the four-cylinder battlefield: the GPZ 900 R (note the capital Z in the model name) had a watercooled, four-valves-per cylinder engine. The one-time company policy of sticking to air-cooling and two-valve heads was abandoned. This new bike was setting standards in 1983: it was the modern bike,

no doubt whatever. It was also the best sports bike. The integral fairing on this model was new for Kawasaki. The GPZ 750 Turbo was an exercise in styling that reached a peak in the GPZ 900 R. The faired Honda CX 500 Turbo was earlier on the scene; but the Kawasaki fairing, made clear that motorcycles and fairings should be designed together. The standard in quality was defined: what had passed muster in the previous decade was no longer good enough. The 900's 115bhp engine meant that this bike was even faster than the already super-quick GPz 1100. More than 150mph could be achieved. The Uni-Trak rear suspension broke with

tradition also. The bike was totally new. And so well built, with superb handling and amazing braking! John Bloor picked this bike as a case study for his Triumph engineers. A GPZ 900 R was taken apart and examined and analysed for as long as was needed to fully understand the design; then he embarked on a modular programme of triples and fours of different capacities, all on the basis of the Kawasaki. Even the frame was part of the exercise: 'undress' a Kawa and a Triumph, and you'll see what I mean. When Triumphs appeared on the market, the Kawasaki was still around. Both Kawasakis and Triumphs were good machines, and made it into the nineties.

There were no problems at all with the new generation of Kawasakis: so why not classic status for them? Perhaps because two models that were far more revolutionary hit the market a year later. The Yamaha FZ 750 and the Suzuki GSX R 750 overshadowed – there's no better word – the

Kawasaki, although that did not stop the 900 Ninja being very successful. In fact it's true to say that the successors to the 900 were less successful than the original. There was the GPZ 1000 RX, and after that the ZX 10 Tomcat. Ever more powerful, but not so successful. The original 900 will outlive them. The 1000cc bikes were pure sports machines. They had to cope with delectable numbers like the Yamaha FZR 1000 and the Suzuki GSX R 1100. It was the ZZR 1100 that restored the Kawasaki to a top position. Not in engineering; in fact even now this has not been achieved by Kawasaki – but in sheer performance. As with the old Z 1, ostensibly less advanced technology can deliver power. A ZZR 1100 has 156bhp on tap, and, you'd better believe, this is one fast bike! The ZZRs can be considered the true followers of the GPZ 900 R Ninja. The ZZR range (a 600 followed the 1100) developed into sports tourers, rather than out and out sports bikes. The sports angle was to be taken up by the ZXR 750.

The late eighties Zephyr models, from 550 to 1100cc (this one is a 750), are presently known as retro bikes. Source of inspiration is the Z 1 of 1973. A Zephyr easily outperforms the Z 1 but does not have its charisma.

Four-valve, water-cooled 1984 Kawasaki GPZ 900 R marked a radical new technical departure for his maker. The 900 was followed by many similar models.

Like Honda's RC 30, the ZXR 750 was mainly designed as a production racer, but was less expensive than the Honda. The green, white and grey Kawasaki beauty succeeded in keeping up with the GSX-R and the FZ. Technically less advanced, as far as refined engine construction is concerned, the Kawasaki made up for that shortfall by going for a higher state of tune. All other ZXR features are absolutely A1. The strong, well-designed E-box frame is as good as the Deltabox frame of the

Yamaha. The Suzuki's frame is less sophisticated than that of the other two. In Superbike racing, the Kawasakis were even more successful than the opposition. Pure power, you see …

The off-road sector, initially a difficult field for Kawasaki, was finally blessed with the KLR 500 and, later, the 600. The engines of this pair were indeed remarkable: dohc, watercooled, and very advanced. They were close to the mighty Yamaha XTs and Honda XLs; technically, they were even superior. The end of the decade saw capacity grow to 650cc, and the number of variations on the theme was bewildering. The all-road sector that had been 'forgotten' by Kawasaki was now filled by the Tengai, a KLX 650 derivative. Honda Transalp, Yamaha Ténéré and Suzuki DR 750 Big were making the running here, in that order. A parallel-twin KLE 500 was not overly successful. The GTR 1000, a GPZ 900 R sibling, turned out to be a lasting model a shafty that turned into a cheaper competitor for Honda's Pan-European and the BMW K 100 RT. The others were more advanced, but the GTR's price tag ensured the Kawasaki's place in the market. There was a Gold Wing challenger as well: the Z 1300 Voyager six-cylinder had everything a Wing could offer. The Kawasaki, even bigger and heavier than the Honda,

The 1986 Kawasaki ZX 10 Tomcat was a 1000cc variant of the GPZ 900 R. It had more power but lacked the balanced looks of the 900. ZX 10 will be forgotten when the older 900 will still be revered.

was able to put 116mph on the digital speedometer, which was more than a Honda could manage. (Nobody seemed very impressed.) The Voyager stayed as an exclusive, modest seller; the Gold Wing was the big seller.

The custom field in which Kawasaki had had such a bad start was home to a better bet from big K. People seemed to want V-twins. And plenty of cubes. OK, here we are: the VN 15 Vulcan – 1500 cc big enough? It was a watercooled V-twin with double camshafts in each head. Two camchains per head made it possible to have the cams close together. Why? They had to be hidden. The water-cooling, too, was played down: the Vulcan came over as an aircooled, simple V-twin. There were balance shafts in the crankcase, following the Yamaha TX 750 example. So the big 1500 hardly vibrated at all. Nor did the 750 Vulcan. The VN looked like a Harley, but didn't sound or feel like a H-D. A Vulcan had more power, handled better and had better brakes. Many people were happy with the VN models from Kawasaki. The Vulcans battled in the market place with Honda Shadows, Yamaha Viragos and Suzuki Intruders. All were V-twins. In the end, the Intruder was the most distinctive model.

The smaller parallel twins, like the Z 305 LTD and the Z 454 LTD, continued unnoticed in the product line. Between the real customs and the sports bikes, there were the Eliminator machines – ZL 600, 900 and, later, the 1000 four-cylinders that were inspired by drag racers. Honda's Magna and the Yamaha V-Max were what the Eliminator series was up against. Suzuki had nothing in this area. The Yamaha V Max beat them all.

However, Kawasaki were successful in the retro-bike field, adapting the styling of the Z 1 900 of 1973 in a GPz-based mixture of old and modern techniques to produce 550, 750 and 1100cc models under the general title of Zephyr. The so-called retro-bike finds plenty of followers among motorcyclists who, scorning the look of truly modern bikes, can still benefit from the achievements of modern technology while enjoying the memories of the Z they used to ride. Alongside the Zephyrs, Kawasaki relaunched the GPZ 900 R and the even older GPz 400. The Z 550 and 750 GT workhorses too were reborn. Their low price made them fair sellers. Are these bikes the ultimate UJMs? If you are looking for a reliable, everyday machine, you can not choose better.

SUZUKI IN THE EIGHTIES

Like Kawasaki, Suzuki got off to a good start in the 1980s. The GS series, in 500, 550, 750, 850 and 1000cc capacities, was well received by the public. The bikes were indeed very good and the GS 1000 was fast, as well as being a good bike. It lacked charisma, but could win any battle with its contemporaries, both in handling and speed. Even the CB X, the acknowledged class leader, was beaten on the road (if not on the drag strip). The GS 850 was Suzuki's early attempt to turn out a tourer. This unburstable machine, with its shaft drive, gained a place in the market behind the Gold Wing from

Kawasaki GTR 1000. Another touring variation on the GPZ 900 R theme. Because it is cheaper than other more luxurious tourers it manages to stay in the sales lists.

(below) The 1500cc VN 15 Vulcan is Kawasaki's answer to Honda's Shadow range. The vee-twin engine is the biggest twin-cylinder around. Torque, from the bottom of the rev range, is enormous.

Honda. None of the shaft-drive tourers from Suzuki handled well, including the 850's big brother, the GS 1000 G, or the GS 650 GT.

The original GS 750, too, maintained a good place in the market. There was no feature of particular merit to be discerned in this machine; it was, however, so extremely well built, so utilitarian, that it sold in huge numbers, just like the Honda CB 400 F in the seventies. If we were to make comparisons with cars, in the case of the GS 750, it would be with a Volkswagen Beetle, arguably a far better car than a Ferrari. (Although, of course, everybody would choose a Ferrari, given the choice!)

The big tourers and the customs were not, initially, catered for in Suzuki's model range. The GS 400 L and GS 550 L soft choppers remained unnoticed. The Hondas did better here. Off-road was another area where Suzuki had little success. The terrible SP 370 was followed by the DR 400 S which was a little better than the SP, but even the DR 500 S was not in the same ballpark as an XT 500 or an XL 500.

In 1981, Suzuki managed to take a notable step forward with the GSX 750 and 1100, which gave Suzuki an identity of its own. Technology had advanced: there were four valves per cylinder now,

and the special combustion chamber Suzuki had developed made the engine more efficient. The TSCC (Twin Swirl Combustion Chamber) did not create that much more power, but it's a fact that the rather raw engines became far smoother. The bulkier styling of the GSX range was not well received, but punters bought the bikes anyway. In fact, the GSX 750 and 1100 models were a great success – the only competing line to challenge the Kawasaki fours in sales.

Though very happy with the technical standard of the GSX models, Suzuki were not convinced they had achieved striking looks. The German design firm Target Design was approached, and the result was rather radical. The Katana was born. It was a purely cosmetic change, and something of a culture shock. It was as if a photograph of a bike had been cut into pieces, and then the pieces glued together by a drunk or a little child! Fierce discussions arose between fanatical supporters and critics of the Katana. You were either strongly against, or in support of, the new bike. We shall see Katana influences on view in later bikes, of Suzuki manufacture and from competitors. The styling was honoured by the 1994 rebirth of the GSX 1100

Kawasaki's KLX 600 is one of the few off road singles that features double overhead camshafts.

KLE 650 from Kawasaki, as a parallel twin, is rather an oddball among allroaders. The engine is wide for such a model; there's sporty performance, however...

Katana, intended as a tribute to the 1982 1100 Katana. Suzuki wisely kept normal models in production as well; customers could choose just what they wanted. Sales were good. The off-road sector, in which, as I've said, Suzuki were not so successful, was indirectly responsible for that distinctive all-roads bike, the DR 750 (later DR 800) Big, which was a single! The biggest single in production, in fact. It was not meant as a dirt-bike, and could be seen as a competitor for the Honda Transalp and the Ténéré from Yamaha. The 'bird's beak' styling gave it a special look.

One might expect such a big single as the DR to be a slow-revving, torquey machine. Not so: this one needs to be revved! Shift down and go – that was, and is, what the DR is all about. The ultra short stroke was mainly responsible for this characteristic. In sharp contrast to the tall DR Big was the LS 650 Savage custom. That one, too, was a single but the engine was very different, having plenty of low-speed torque. The LS probably had the lowest saddle height of any contemporary. The Savage was an original custom with its own face. All these successful derivatives of the DR off-roaders showed

that Suzuki could make very effective singles. Custom bikes were difficult for Suzuki at first. The Savage was followed by the even more successful Intruder range. Very soon these models were at the top of the custom sales lists. A V-twin in 600, 700, 750, 800 and 1,400cc sizes forms the heart of the bike. Not much effort was made to give the Intruder a Harley look. They are far slimmer. However, the Intruder was accused of being a copy of the Harley. You might imagine that the bike is very 'simple'. Nothing could be further from the truth. The battery is in a box in front of the rear wheel. If ever you want to replace the battery, make sure you have a few hours to spare! The wheel has to be removed, and there is no centre stand! Then there's the business of synchronising the carburettors. They are connected by cables. If you want to adjust the front one you need to do so, somehow, through the rear one. Grrrr! Still, even Harley owners have been known to express some admiration for an Intruder.

The tourers, with Suzuki's four-cylinder shaft-drive GS series, was joined by the GV 1400 Cavalcade. The big V-four of the Cavalcade was specially designed for the bike. It was in essence a 'Suzuki

Suzuki's bread-and-butter model that successfully ledt his maker into the eighties: the GS 550. If the Universal Japanese Motorcycle exists, this is it.

(right) The SP 370 was
Suzuki's failed attempt
to introduce something
new in the off-road
market. It was
unreliable and had no
performance, as well as
no looks! (In spite of
this nice picture from
the sales brochure...)

This square – four
two – stroke RG 500
appeals to Grand Prix
fans. The engine can
be regarded as a
detuned race unit.

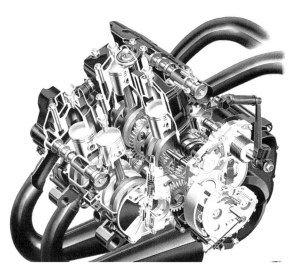

Gold Wing'. And it was a good tourer, but with
nothing to offer that could not be had from a
genuine Gold Wing. And then there was the XN 85
Turbo (more on this one later), followed by the 1985
GSX R 750 and 1100. More about these later, too.
The sporting two-stroke did not die altogether in the
eighties. The RGV 250 and RG 500 were detuned
racers – and not much detuned, at that. The

advanced two-strokes were as fast as a 750 or an
1100. Of course, they were not suitable for everyday
commuting, tending to wear out early and burning a
lot of fuel. But what exciting bikes they were! That
dream, to own a licensed racer, could come true. The
250 was a V-twin, the 500 a square-four. Yamaha
were the big challengers, with the RD 350 LC
parallel twin, and the RD 500 LC, like the Suzuki, a

Suzuki showed
courage with its 1981
GSX 1100 Katana.
'Target Design' styling
inspired (together with
the Honda Turbo) the
general looks of so
many bikes of the
eighties and nineties.

Single cylinder Suzuki LS 650 has a reputation of being a lady's bike because of the ultra-low seat. It is definitely a bike with some personality.

Suzuki GSX 750 F of 1989: a modern UJM? If a consumer's guide had tested it, this machine would have been awarded a Best Buy accolade. One's heart is not touched by it, however.

VS 1400 Intruder was one of the most successful vee-twin custom bikes. Even among Harley owners it gained some credibility, although of course H-D remains number one in 'Custom Country'.

square-four. The Yamahas won on reliability, the Suzukis on speed. Kawasaki had a tandem-twin two-stroke KR 250, a direct derivative of their very successful GP racer. And Honda, with the NSR 400 triple, showed that the pre-eminent four-stroke manufacturer found this category of machines interesting enough to have a go. None of these two-strokes was a big seller, but they were good for the manufacturer's image. Lovely playthings...
Suzuki followed Kawasaki in the naked-bike arena with the GSX 1100 G, a detuned GSX R 1100

without the fairing and the war colours. A shaft drive replaced the chain, torque was enormous and the handling good. The fast version was already acknowledged as a good bike; the detuned G model seemed to be absolutely bulletproof. However, although 'detuned', it would do 160mph – if you could stay aboard! Its looks were reminiscent of those of the GS 850 from the start of the decade. Many people buy a 'naked' bike to fit a fairing – it's true! The fact that it is cheaper then a full-dress bike is one reason for this apparently illogical step.

Suzuki's Intruders, too, came out in 'all-rounder' guise. The VX 800 was what you might call a no-nonsense bike. The engine had been tuned a little to make it more aggressive than in Intruder form. It is a challenger to Honda's NVT 650 Revere. The latter is the better machine, especially in the handling department, but both bikes are capable of much more than you would think. Modest power figures quoted in their sales literature do not exactly promise high performance, but can be misleading. The superb handling and the smooth way the power is put to the ground make a VX able to outperform much stronger machines, particularly on twisting B roads.

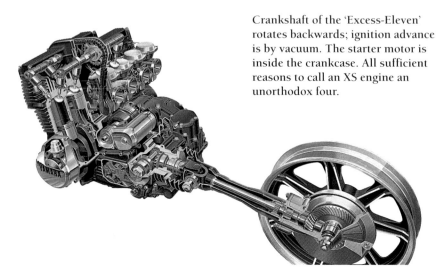

Crankshaft of the 'Excess-Eleven' rotates backwards; ignition advance is by vacuum. The starter motor is inside the crankcase. All sufficient reasons to call an XS engine an unorthodox four.

YAMAHA IN THE EIGHTIES

Yamaha had just climbed out of a 'down' period when the 1980s appeared on the calendar. Not as depressing as Suzuki's experience, perhaps, but Yamaha had suffered mishaps in the 1970s. The once-successful RD 125, 200, 250 and 400cc aircooled two-strokes were outdated by 1980 and the XS 360, 400 and 500 four-stroke twins did not make any significant impression. The 750 triple four-stroke, the XS 750, was pretty lousy. Simply: it was not fast enough for the money and the capacity. The first four-cylinder from Yamaha, the XS 1100, was a good machine, although large and bulky. It was very sturdy and quite fast, with its shaft drive giving it a touring character. A peculiarity of the engine was that it ran backwards, which could be inconvenient if you forgot while timing the camshafts! Another peculiarity: the location of the starter motor on the inside of the upper crankcase, which meant that if ever there was a problem with it, such as worn brushes, you needed to strip the entire engine. Fortunately, the starter gave little trouble; indeed the XS 1100's reliability record in general was excellent. The 1100 found supporters, but a Kawasaki Z 1000, Z 1 R or a Suzuki GS 1000 were easier to sell. The looks of the XS Eleven were, well, not appreciated; yet the bike had to lead for Yamaha. In sales, the XT 500 and the XS 650 kept

The 1977 XS 1100 was the first four-cylinder four-stroke from Yamaha. After the firm's unhappy start with the XS 750 triple, this model came as a relief: it was OK. Later XJ models based on the XS were successful in the eighties.

Suzuki's retro bike: the GSX 1100 G is, as far as styling is concerned, based on... the Kawasaki Z 1 of 1973. Detuned GSX R engine is totally bulletproof and far more advanced than the power units of other retro bikes.

(left) The XS 750 had a bad start, but the later 850cc triple had all the troubles sorted out. The bike also had the 'go' that the 750 lacked. John Bloor's Triumph triples show that Yamaha should have kept the three-cylinder model in the sales lists.

Yamaha afloat. The XJ 400, 550, 650, 750, and 900 four-cylinders were of excellent quality. They performed well, and they lasted. Their styling was conservative. They were not precisely bestsellers, but they sold in reasonable numbers. In the end, the XJ 900 turned out to be almost everlasting, becoming

something of a symbol of reliability. It soldiered on into the 90s, to be followed by the more or less similar 900 Diversion.

The custom field is another story for Yamaha. The established XS 650 SE was quite successful, but the 1981 XV 750 Virago aircooled V-twin was the first of the customs to really hit the big time. The XV could be described as 'two XTs on one crankcase'. The engine was very pleasant, and final drive was by shaft. Maintenance was simple, and not much of it was required. There was only one complaint: the starter motor made the same noises as the starter on the old TX 750 and XS 650 models, and often broke down. But when this happened, it was easy to repair – so, really, it wasn't a big problem. And in the final versions of the bike the snag was completely eliminated. Kawasaki used in-line fours in their customs, as did Suzuki. All the manufacturers restricted their parallel twins to small capacities. The only really successful competitor for the XVs from Yamaha was the Honda CX 500 Custom.

An XV 1000 Midnight Special is still a good-looking

Yamaha was the first Japanese manufacturer to find the right shape for custom bikes, with this 1981 XV 1000 Midnight Special. Later, Virago models followed his styling.

Yamaha XJ 900 can be seen as a UJM, but this machine has been around for more than a decade, into the nineties. The same applies to XJ 400, 550, 600, 650 and other capacity models.

The 1987 FJ 1200 was, with the intervening FJ 1100, a follower of the XS 1100. The frame of the FJ, with the steering head buttressed by the frame tubes, was rather special. Initially considered a sports machine, the model survived as a sporty tourer.

bike even ten years or more after it first appeared. All the XV models were grouped under the name of Virago in the late 80s. The range was extended, of course, since it was so successful. In the end even the little parallel twins, down to the 250, were replaced by V-twin Viragos. The 1000cc TR 1 all-rounder, based on the XV engine, launched at the beginning of the 80s, was soon abandoned after rejection by the public. The unsprung rear mudguard was ugly, it's true, but the motorcycle as a whole was of outstanding quality. But … no sale. The original winning bike of the seventies for Yamaha, the small two-stroke, was rediscovered by the company; the 1981 RD 350 LC was a watercooled successor to the old aircooled RD 400, and was in fact a close derivative of the TZ racers Yamaha sold for clubman's racing. It was a 350 that could outperform many old 750s. RD 350 LC cup racing did a lot of good for the model, helping it to become popular among youth with racing in the blood but little money in the pocket. When the other makers (including Honda) came out with race-bred two-strokes, Yamaha went one step

further, selling their square-four RD 500 LC as a Grand Prix bike with a licence plate. The impact of these bikes was enormous. It has been mentioned, but I'd repeat that there was one more sector in which Yamaha started out with high expectations. The off-road XT 500 was firmly in the lead, with the 1979 and 1980 Paris-Dakar rallies falling to that model. Later, the expensive factory machines and teams would keep the privateers and 'ordinary' bikes out of the reckoning. But before that happened, you needed an XT if you were to compete in off-road sport. Development continued, with the more modern XT 550 ready to follow the 500. It finally appeared; but that did not mean the end of the 500. The 550 had a longer suspension travel, more power and more sophistication, all needed to compete with the modern Honda XL 500. The Suzuki and Kawasaki off-road machines did not count. Soon, there was a whole range of four-stroke off-roaders, from 125 to 600cc. All these models did well, even the smaller ones. Derivatives such as the Ténéré were inspired by the factory specials that disputed the Paris-Dakar in later years. Huge fuel tanks were trademarks of these bikes. World explorers benefited from the developments, because no longer did they

(right) **In the way that the RD 500 was a roadgoing racer, this Yamaha V-Max is a roadgoing dragster, with 145bhp to shred the rear tyre.**

Design error and correction, as illustrated by the Yamaha TR 1. The old version was meant as a sort of modern-day Vincent. Wrong: leave the Vincent alone, please! The later version was a better attempt at an all-round bike.

In 1984 Yamaha showed that the two-stroke could be hi-tech: this RD 500 LC was a worthy competitor to the RG 500 of Suzuki. Both models can be seen as roadgoing racers; the Yamaha was the slightly more civilised of the two.

have to think only of a BMW for their trip! A Yamaha would do the job. Enduro competition also found Yamaha represented on the front row, for the TT 600 was the only worthy competitor to the dominant Honda XR 600. However, all these developments were largely ignored by the legions that stuck to the original XT 500! The last 500 rolled off the assembly line as late as 1989. The touring sector was a different story for Yamaha, where dominance was claimed by the Honda Gold Wing. The 1200cc Yamaha XVZ 12 TD Venture did nothing to change that. Its V-four engine was good, but Yamaha underwent the same fate as the Suzuki Cavalcade and the Kawasaki Voyager in competition with the big Honda. The Gold Wing was unbeatable, and that was that.

Initially, the market for the sporting four-cylinder motorcycle was a difficult one for Yamaha. But then, with the FJ 1100, the company found a way to impress. This modern version of the XS 1100 had all the peculiarities of the original sorted out. There was fresh styling for the heavy but fine-handling sports bike. The frame was a novelty: Yamaha called it the Lateral Frame Concept. The steering head was built in a different way, being 'surrounded' by the frame, to contribute great rigidity. When this was combined with good suspension – and it was – the FJ 1100 became an outstanding bike. All the objections that had kept the XS 1100 from being a success had been eliminated. Initial sales were not spectacular; but the 1100 was here to stay. Soon the focus changed from pure sports to sports tourer, and the capacity grew to 1200cc. The FJ 1200 turned

out to be an 'evergreen' motorcycle, on sale way into the 1990s. Each year it became more popular, like the Kawa GPZ 900 R and Honda's CBR 1000. Yamaha was also outstanding in bringing out that milestone in motorcycle history, the FZ, in 1985. The GSX-R series from Suzuki and the FZs from Yamaha were to be the technical basis of the following generation of sports bikes.

Yamaha was going strong, anyway, with another winner. The Venture tourer lent its engine to the drag racer-inspired 145bhp V-Max. The handling of the V-Max was mediocre, and so was the riding position. But nobody cared. This was the ultimate boulevard cruiser. It could be entered in the 'ultimate street bike' class in drag racing and you'd stand a good chance of winning! Styling was extreme, for it had to look like a drag racer. Fortunately, it also performed like one. I once saw one leave the parking place of a drag race at 50mph. The rider wanted to show off. He shifted gear and pulled the throttle wide open. The rear wheel spun, leaving a black strip of rubber on the tarmac a hundred feet long. The shaft drive would take this sort of abuse without complaint. Later, I understood that this treatment was nothing special for a V-Max. All you had to do was peg the revs at 1500rpm, and open up. No hesitation whatever – just go! Forget about the gearbox. A joy at traffic lights. The Kawasaki Eliminator does all kinds of things, but eliminating a V-Max is not one of them. Even Yamaha itself could not improve on the bike. The smaller FZ-based FZX 750 Fazer followed the TR 1 into early retirement. End of story: the Max survives alone.

The five Turbos were very different, one from another, in behaviour. They were the outcome of a battle for prestige, initiated by Honda.

By the end of the decade Yamaha achieved a dream they had cherished since the 1960s. They were the biggest motorcycle manufacturer in the world!

TURBOS
■ ■ AN INTERESTING ■ ■
DEAD END

Rare sight: all the Japanese production turbo motorcycles photographed together. In the early eighties many people believed that motorcycles of the future would be turbocharged. But they were wrong...

In the seventies manufacturers were selling special kits to install on motorcycles to get more power. In the world of cars, this was common practice. The turbo goes back to pre-war days. Many piston-engined aircraft had turbos. A Kawasaki Z 1000 or a Suzuki GS 1000 modified with a turbo would easily gain 20mph in top speed. KKK and Rajay were two of the manufacturers. Drag-racing machines performed in an unbelievable way. I know of a 1400cc CB X with two turbos. The whole quarter-mile is run on the rear wheel, with the front wheel not turning at all. And the sound …

It was Kawasaki America that first came out with a limited series of 'production' Z 1 R turbos. Cooling and lubrication problems inhibited success. A Kawasaki engine runs on rather low oil pressure, because of the ball bearings favoured in its construction. A turbo wants a real flood of oil under high pressure, because they run very hot and the rotational speed of the shaft can exceed 200,000rpm. Yet the point was made about turbos, despite the difficulties. Ten years before, everybody was talking of Wankels: now the turbo was in view. By then the power race had just begun. It was Honda that made a point of being the first to launch a turbo motorcycle, with an aircooled 360cc prototype of a V-twin turbo engine dating back to 1973. The Kawasaki turbo of the Americans stung them! The

benefits of a turbo were loss of weight and power gain. It should be possible to take a small bike and give it the power of a big machine. Fuel consumption would improve. Exhaust gasses would be cleaner.

HONDA CX 500 TC

In 1981 Honda announced the CX 500 TC Turbo in a blaze of publicity. It was indeed a courageous attempt to redefine the motorcycle. The TC had fuel injection, with a multitude of sensors checking various conditions in the engine and sending the information to a computer: pressure before and after the turbo, exhaust gases, position of the throttle, detonation; that sort of thing. The computer controlled the fuel injection as well as the ignition. On paper, technically speaking, the CX 500 was perfect. Compression was low, to enable the turbo to blow. There was a backup system for when the computer noticed a problem; then it would take standard settings, and not change them, which would enable the rider to get home, and to the dealer, where the computer would relay information on the nature of the failure which had occurred, to a

well-read mechanic. However, the whole business with a computer was too new for the general motorcycling public, which basically refused to pay extra for a complicated motorcycle that could be outclassed by a normal 1100. Road-test reports made clear that the CX 500 Turbo was a case of overkill. The sensors often caused the computer to feed the injectors too much fuel. The knocking sensor for detonation made the Turbo thirsty. Turbo lag – the hesitation of the engine before the turbo

Honda CX 500 TC is not so responsive to the throttle at lower revs, when the turbo is not working. The numerous sensors in the injection management system contribute to the 500's thirst.

Turbo components: the 180,000rpm inner shaft, the wastegate for excess pressure, the snail-shaped housing...

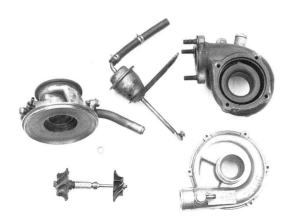

Yamaha XJ 650 Turbo would today be a good tourer, with its rather bulky fairing. The right exhaust is only heard when the wastegate is open.

comes on steam – was too noticeable. However, the integrated fairing of the TC was highly appreciated. It was pointing towards future styling, as the electronics did for engine management. Ten years later, computers on board motorcycles are commonplace. The CX 500 Turbo would have been more successful if it had not been priced at almost twice the going figure for a normal machine. It was a case of too little performance for too much money.

■ ▨ Riding the CX 500 Turbo ▨ ■

The exhaust note was quiet, for a turbo also serves as an extra muffler. At low revs, the bike felt reluctant to accelerate, as if one cylinder wasn't firing. Engine response was tardy as the throttle was blipped – a little like a Suzuki rotary. When you opened the throttle wide, the reaction was wild! The normal CX 500 had slow reaction to the right wrist. The seat was comfortable: in its day the Turbo was meant as a sports bike, but it was in fact a comfortable sports tourer, with the absence of exhaust noise emphasising this fact. The absolutely perfect fairing was responsible for long journeys being a joy on this bike, when you could open the throttle, and the gentle tourer would become something of a beast. The effect was not so abrupt as with a Kawasaki 750 Mach 4, but there was definitely a difference when the turbo kicked in. Nowadays, if you ride a CX Turbo, the ease it has in reaching 125mph will make you forget that this is a bike that's more than 15 years old. In fact, it's too civilised. With a turbo, surely you want to be thrilled? Handling, though, is good. The brakes are not really very impressive.

YAMAHA'S TURBO

Only a few months later, Yamaha came up with an answer to the CX Turbo. The XJ 650 Turbo followed a simpler technology path than the Honda. The compression ratio was almost the same as in the XJ 650 from which the Turbo was derived. The carburettors were left in place, being 30mm constant-vacuum instruments. The exhausts of a Yamaha Turbo are strange: the right one only makes a sound when the wastegate opens to let off the surplus of pressure; exhaust gasses all pass through the left muffler. The Yamaha, like the TC, had a

fairing designed integrally with the rest of the bike. Taste of course is always something to argue about; but the square looks of Yamaha's effort do not really appeal. The fairing is rather tourist orientated, as well. Good for a touring machine, of course, but as an eye catcher this Turbo asks for something more exotic.

■ ▨ Riding the Yamaha XJ 650 Turbo ▨ ■

The first impression the Yamaha gives is of a 'normal' motorcycle. There's no distinctive styling, as with the Honda. Of course, there are novel details … The fueltank, for one, hidden under a cover. The XJ, ridden in the 90s, strikes one as being very comfortable. The seat is even more receptive than the Honda's. As soon as you start the Yamaha, you get a feeling how your ride will be. The four-cylinder sounds a little raw, and the turbo whines. The bikes feels absolutely normal when it's ridden slowly. At low revs, you feel there are more horses available than in Honda's 500 TC. If the bike is made to work, and you go for the red zone before you shift up, the bike shows the sporting character you were expecting. It just keeps on going. And the

exhaust note matches your speed. Now you are riding a Turbo! Test reports used to mention a big difference in performance between the Honda and the Yamaha. In fact, the bikes have different personalities but their performance is close. That the Yamaha's handling is so good is strange, for the frame is not that much different from other Yamahas'. My conclusion: the Yamaha is a good machine, giving a nice exhaust sound. But overall it is not exciting enough for the prestige battle in which the Turbos of the 1980s participated.

Suzuki XN 85 Turbo

Then Suzuki produced a turbo. They had gone to even less trouble than the others to make an entry in the new class. The bike even looked rather conventional. Katana styling elements were used, but in a restrained way. The fairing of the XN was smaller than that of the other bikes, and the seat more overtly sporting than those of the first two Turbos I have discussed. The fact that Suzuki was not perhaps very involved in their Turbo can be seen in its low turbo-pressure.

Suzuki XN 85 was the sleekest of the five Turbos. Styling was based on the Katana. But there was no real 'turbo-kick'.

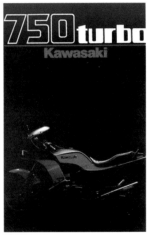

(top) **The CX 500 may have been technically the most advanced Turbo, but on the road the Kawasaki is arguably the most balanced machine. Its styling was a source of inspiration for Kawasakis in the second part of the eighties.**

Testers had no high regard for the Suzuki. One point has to be emphasised, however. The injection of the Suzuki Turbo worked well, even when the bike was idling; a real achievement. No bike with injection is able to tickover in a decent way. Not even modern machines. Even that futuristic bike, the Yamaha GTS 1000, does not run properly below 1200rpm. The Suzuki did …

■ ▨ Riding the Suzuki XN 85 Turbo ▨ ■

There have been very few Suzuki turbos. It is the most anonymous: at first sight these days, it strikes one as a cross between the grey GSX 1100 of 1982 and a Katana. It is a bike without an identity. Only from the front is there some sign of aggression. The exhaust sound is absolutely normal. The sporty seat and handling make for a nice sports bike, and the XN is slim and low. If you were to close your eyes, you would get the impression that you were riding a GSX 600 F. This turbo is willing to approach 125mph; but it takes a little time. The engine will even stop pulling before the red zone is reached, which is very un-turbo-like. Since the Suzuki is a four-cylinder, any comparison with the Honda seems rather pointless. But comparing Suzuki and Yamaha makes some sense. Overall, the performance of the

Sales brochure of the Kawasaki GPZ 750 Turbo: 'The last, the best'. A statement that is open to challenge...

bikes does not differ that much. The Suzuki takes off at low revs, better than the Yamaha. It also handles better. Yet the Yamaha excites where the Suzuki remains just a rather fast but 'normal' machine. Suzuki did not make an impression in the turbo world. They were there; but that's about it. For collectors, it may be the most desirable, for it is very rare indeed.

KAWASAKI GPZ 750 TURBO

It was already 1983 when the Kawasaki came out. The expensive sales brochure speaks of 'The last, the best Turbo'. It was considered the fastest production motorcycle at the time. Kawasaki had the benefit of the experience of the others and had done their homework, analysing all the disadvantages of the competing bikes. To begin with, the Kawasaki had 100cc more capacity, and the initial compression ratio was close to that of a normal engine. Its well

designed and very logical construction made the Kawasaki the best-built four-cylinder turbo. Testers of the day agreed with the claims laid out in the sales brochure. Much effort had been put into the chassis, and the fairing was a real work of art. Only Honda's styling ranks as being more advanced. As to performance, at low revs there is plenty of power and the bike really goes when pushed hard. But by 1983 the question had arisen as to whether the world was really waiting for turbos. Kawasaki gave the answer themselves: their GPZ 900 R was faster and handled better than all the turbo bikes! And it was easier to maintain, and cheaper to buy.

■ ▨ Riding the GPZ 750 Turbo ▨ ■

Honda had made a statement with their turbo. Yamaha and Suzuki were there to make sure they were not left out. But Kawasaki wanted to win the race. The 112bhp of their turbo shamed the others. The Kawasaki's turbo was visible in the front of the fairing, and looked interesting, even exciting! If you try one now, you find that it handles very well. The 'go' is there from the start and remains until revs are well into the red zone. You need a very good 1100 to keep up with this turbo. Braking matches the power. The exhaust makes clear what kind of bike you are riding. This Kawasaki is fast; and it can be made even faster. There is a different chip for the ignition that can be obtained – or you used to be able to obtain – from Kawasaki. The wastegate can be re-adjusted to open later. Then the turbo starts behaving like a two-stroke, and when you shift into top gear on full power the front wheel will lift. The wastegate of the Kawasaki is the only one of the turbos that can be heard, which adds to the fun.

The Kawasaki is smoother than the Yamaha, giving the impression that the Yamaha is faster, but in fact the reverse is true.

THE HONDA CX 650 TC
THE LAST ONE

Honda definitely wanted the last word in the turbo world. Criticism of the CX 500 Turbo had stung the management. It was 1984 when the CX 650 saw the light. Capacity was bigger, compression ratio higher. This took care of the turbo-lag from which the 500 suffered. Electronics were simplified a little, with fewer sensors to influence the computer. The manual choke was back. Slightly different styling, and omission of one colour, distinguished the 650 from the 500. The main, blue, colour gave the bike an exciting look (on the 500 grey was the main colour). The fairing was made in PVC, leading to a weight reduction. Test riders spoke of a very good touring bike. The press did not make comparisons with other turbos but confined itself to pointing out the big improvement over the CX 500 TC. The 650 had better fuel economy, but still was a thirsty machine, according to the testers.

Honda CX 650 TC had simplified injection management as well as an extra 100cc over the 500. Unexpected bonus was that it outperformed the Kawasaki.

■ ■ Riding the CX 650 TC ■ ■

Even today, you might think a four-in-line engine is better suited for turbocharging than a vee-twin. The first few miles on a 650 might seem to confirm this belief. But that first impression is deceptive. Minor cycle-part modifications, like the inclusion of a front-fork bridge, make the 650 feel tighter on the road. The 650 initially feels like a 500 when at normal pace but when, say, a car is overtaken on a dual carriageway the difference becomes evident. You need not down-shift! The 650 simply takes off when you twist the throttle. So, indisputably, the 650 is faster than the 500. How does it stack up against a Kawasaki Turbo? Guess what! The Honda out-accelerates the Kawasaki! The CX 650 Turbo does not sound exciting, like the Kawasaki. Maybe a Kawasaki would regain some terrain on the other side of 125mph? I doubt it. If rather better brakes could be added to this Honda, it would be a perfect all-round touring motorcycle for today. It is both gentle and fast. It can be ridden at tickover engine speeds and revved in the red zone. It will come back for more.

Honda, who started this race, had the last word after all – but by then it was too late. Only a few months later, the Kawasaki GPZ 900 R, the Yamaha FZ 750 and the Suzuki GSX R 750 showed that it wasn't necessary to indulge in complex and expensive turbo techniques to achieve high performance and low weight in a modern motorcycle. Although both the Honda CX 650 TC and the Kawasaki 750 Turbo remained available until 1987, they never sold in any quantity. Still, the turbos have left some influences on the modern motorcycle. Anti-dive front forks have now vanished, but they may well come back one day. The next item is the fairing that is designed integrally with the bike and, last but not least, electronic motor management. The computer, that seemed so alien on the first CX 500 Turbo, is now commonplace, and accepted. Electronic injection is yet another feature we will see more and more. The CX 500 TC (and the Suzuki Katana, by the way) also influenced the styling of many later motorcycles. Even today, if a Honda Turbo is parked among modern bikes it does not look particularly old.

difficult to pinpoint those few machines that really excelled. The general standard of quality was very high. Yamaha's FZ 750 and the Suzuki GSX-R 750 were, however, exceptional. Both appeared in 1985, a little more than a year after Kawasaki's GPZ 900 R, the machine that made it clear that turbocharged motorcycles were dead in the water. Normally aspirated machines could deliver as much power as was desired, while maintaining usability and durability. They were cheaper, too. For Kawasaki, the

YAMAHA FZ750 AND SUZUKI GSX-R750
SPORTS BIKES REDESIGNED

In the 1980s all the makers had so many different bikes on sale, in all sorts of categories, that it is

(top and botom)
The 1985 Yamaha FZ 750 made all other contemporary motorcycles, except one, outdated. It was almost as revolutionairy as the Honda CB 750 had been in 1969.

watercooled 16-valve GPZ 900 R was a radical departure, in view of the company's belief in air-cooled two-valves-per-cylinder fours. The 900 handled as if it was made in Europe at a time when Japanese bikes still had the reputation of being poor handlers, although in fact this was no longer the case. The GPZ made the point, once and for all....

■ ▨ New standard ▨ ■

Now there was Yamaha with the all-new FZ 750. In GP Formula One car racing in the early eighties Yamaha had developed an extremely high revving vee-eight racing engine having no fewer than five valves per cylinder. At the time this engine was really top of the pile, and so somebody at Yamaha thought: "What if we took one half of such an engine and made it the power unit for a motorcycle?" The car engine had a proven reliability record. The valves could be made very light, requiring weaker return springs; power losses would be cut. In theory, six valves to each cylinder

would have been even better; Maserati had tried this in 1969, but without particular success; and when Yamaha went down the same road they found there were no advantages over the five-valve setup, which indeed appeared to offer only one slight drawback, in the less than perfect shape of the combustion chamber. Even this minor drawback could have been overcome by using a third camshaft, which would have permitted a better angle for the third inlet valve: but doing this would have been an expensive business, and there would have been some attendant power losses through increased friction.

So it was decided to go ahead with the five-valver in original form. It would effortlessly spin in excess of 12,000rpm for as long as required, without detriment, and churn out more than 100bhp. Watercooled, it ran without any heating problems (in contrast to what used to happen with earlier air-cooled units); it was lighter; and, finally, it was more reliable. Inserting a modified chip in the ignition circuit meant that power could be boosted to a

FZ 750 was good for at least 140 mph has available with total reliability, and with cycle parts to match. Ergonomics were carefully designed, too.

The 1985
Yamaha FZ 750.

Five valves per
cylinder; the first
check was called for at
30,000 miles. This FZ
engine was technically
state of the art.

redesign the cycle parts of the new bike, with the aid of the company's Cad Cam computer programme, which calculated the strength of various components. Most notably, the computer was called in to assess the frame layout that would best cope with the effect of torque from the rear fork in its path to the steering head of the machine; new, wide, rectangular-section steel 'tubes' were used for the frame, which was effectively strengthened by incorporating the ultra-light engine. In addition, large-diameter front-fork legs were specified, as well as a more robust rear fork (with movement controlled by one suspension element).

The engine configuration allowed another improvement over conventional layouts. Fuel weight in the tank of a 'nommal' motorcycle is carried high, towards the front of the machine. This means changing ratio of weight between front and rear as fuel is used, with consequent deleterious effects on handling. And there is the further disadvantage, with a full tank, of an unnecessarily high centre of gravity, which of course adversely affects comering potential. But on the FZ, because the cylinder head is further forward and lower than usual, the front-rear proportioning of weight can be more easily balanced; the centre of gravity will be lower as well. The fuel tank, Yamaha decided, could be placed in the middle of the wheelbase rather than, as before, at the front. Air-filter and fuel container switched positions. All this meant that, either with a full complement of fuel, or just about dry, the FZ handled in pretty well the same way.

Because the engine was so slim, the footrests could be placed lower, without danger of connecting with the tarmac during comering.

On the face of it, then, it may seem that the FZ was the perfect motorcycle; and indeed it was, just about. Its handling remained neutral through corners, it didn't wiggle in long turns ... and it was fast! I remember being disappointed when, riding my 1979 Kawasaki Zl 300, I was overtaken by one of these Yams. I was on one of the fastest standard motorcycles one could buy - and I couldn't catch that 750. When I later rode the FZ I could appreciate for myself that the improvement it displayed over the previous generation of motorcycle was huge. It handled perfectly. And how it would rev! The brakes were good, too.

Of course, development did not come to a full stop with the FZ. After all, we are talking about the Japanese ... In 1987 the steel frame was replaced by the revolutionary Deltabox, an all-alloy layout with a

healthy 130bhp. In effect, this marked the beginning of the 'chip-tuning' phenomenon.

Retaining the forward inclination of the cylinders, from race car practice, provided an opportunity to

Second-generation FZs, like the FZR 1000, had the all-alloy Genesis frame, a further reason for lavishing praise on this model.

cast-alloy steering head. Tubing was replaced by very visible wide-section aluminium 'booms'. It looked more spectacular than the old frame, and was stiffer and lighter. With the new frame came a new model: the FZR 750. Now the fuel tank became truly integral with the chassis. The FZR went to the USA while the FZ continued to be Europe's standby, with the original frame in steel tubing. When the FZR 1000 came along, however, it was only available in alloy-frame form, with the 142bhp engine making it a real flyer.

Secondhand FZ engines are relatively cheap today. They hardly ever give trouble. Cycle parts, too, are widely available, a tribute to the quality of their construction; they may have suffered in accidents but rarely show signs of rusting. The FZ, then, may be expected to rank in the not-too-distant future as a classic.

SUZUKI TOO

Only a few months after Yamaha's FZ appeared, Suzuki levelled the score by introducing that excellent motorcycle, the GSX-R 750.

The Yamaha was the result of deep calculation; the GSX-R signalled a quite different approach. Suzuki had observed that more than a few motorcyclists were altering their machines to match the looks of racing bikes. Owners were making their bikes lighter, meaner and, of course, faster. Suzuki's conclusion was that they should turn out a machine to fulfill the aspirations of these riders. In 1985 Suzuki had the Katana range on the stocks; but the Katanas were, basically, only regular GSX models: it was a more radical bike that the company was aiming for now.

Like Yamaha, Suzuki started virtually from scratch, although the Twin Swirl Combustion Chambers of the GSX were adopted. There were four valves per cylinder, and this arrangement wasn't altered; indeed, the TSCC heads had been shown to be extremely efficient. New camshafts were developed, operating through cam followers much like those found in Honda's Black Bomber. The valves were closed by light coil springs.

Cooling presented some problems. Watercooling, obviously, was the way to go ... or so it appeared. Suzuki, however, had some interesting ideas that

Forced oil cooling and lubrication are principles dating back to World War Two... This is the 1989 Suzuki GSX-R engine, with radial oil-cooler.

harked back to the second world war, when many piston-engined airplanes employed oiling arrangements capable of pumping lubricant through the system in much greater quantity than was absolutely necessary. Piston crowns, cylinder liners and cam trains were smothered in oil and thus remained cool in all circumstances. So, following the wartime example, the GSX-R acquired a cleverly designed oilspray system that was guaranteed to

keep hard-stressed components both lubricated and cool. It was a matter of doing away with radiator, hoses and water pump in exchange for an oil-cooler. To emphasise that this was a special engine, the anthracite-coloured fins on the cylinder and head were very shallow, and of close pitch.

As for the cycle parts, first, the traditional double-cradle frame was made over into an all-alloy version, very much on show. Up to that time aluminium frames had been seen as reserved for racing bikes; using one on the GSX-R represented a big step forward for a roadster. It was very light, contributing little to a total weight for the l00bhp bike of not more than 200kg.

Of course, the Suzuki was fast. It appeared to answer all the requirements of the hard-riding motorcyclist. Perhaps it didn't have the finesse of Yamaha's FZ, but any lack there was made up for in the Suzuki's sheer, raw sports quality. Incidentally, perhaps that light frame was a trifle too light, for it was found that at very high speeds a little weaving could occur, detracting from the Suzuki's otherwise impeccable road manners. The result, in later years, was that the factory introduced a little extra weight and stiffness.

The only rival for the FZ Yamaha was the 1985 GSX-R range from Suzuki. This is a GSX-R 1100; together with the 750 it put Suzuki ahead of the pack. It was 'right' from the start.

In 1986 Suzuki brought out a big brother to the 750 in the form of the 156bhp GSX-R ll00. Comparing the Suzuki and Yamaha offerings just described brings to mind the l970s GT 750 - the Kettle - and Kawasaki's 750 Mach 4 H2. The Kettle, I submit, was the machine that answered the dictates of the mind, while the raw Mach 4 was the bike of the heart. The same reactions apply in the case of the later machines, I think. (Who can fairly talk about the UJM here!) A Yamaha FZ is a superior, well-balanced motorcycle capable of more performance than most riders will ever require. Suzuki's GSX-R is an aggressive sports bike to captivate any rider; it's bursting with the fun factor! This assessment applies more truly to the early versions; as time passed, the GSX-R became more refined. The choice is simple: if you want a well-mannered, 'softer' GSX-R, go for a recent model; if you are after a 'fun' bike, a future classic, seek out one of the early machines.

AND THE OTHERS?

Kawasaki brought out the ZXR 750 as some sort of answer to the pair from Yamaha and Suzuki I've been talking about. It's an echo of the 1960s situation in which the technically inferior TD I C Yamaha managed to beat the more advanced A I R from Kawasaki and Suzuki's TR 250 on the tracks; this surely is the role of the ZXR, with its E-box frame and striking colour schemes. Performance is good - of course - but there is nothing about the bike that

ZXR 750 was Kawasaki's E-box-framed answer to the superfast Yamahas and Suzukis. It even outperformed them on the race tracks. Yet it was technically a conventional design, in contrast to the other two.

suggests a new trend or new developments. It is, in fact, 'just' an extremely well made, conventional hyper-sports motorcycle.

Honda, on the other hand, did make something rather special. Theirs was a difficult job: they had to create a success from the initially troublesome vee-fours. They managed it with the VFR 750 R - also known as RC 30, a red/blue/white warbird with a one-sided rear suspension system. It had power to match the Yamaha and the Suzuki, and could outhandle both on the race circuits ... ask Joey Dunlop! The fact that it costs twice as much as the opposition, while being somewhat short of being twice as good, technically or in performance, precludes it in my opinion from being really significant. Exotic? Yes. Beautiful? Yes. Collectable? Yes. Historically important? No!

SOME THOUGHTS ABOUT THE NINETIES

The motorcycle these days is so very close to perfection that it will have to be redefined, if anything as revolutionary as the CB 750 or FZ 750 Yamaha is to be possible. One machine stands out in this decade: the new BMW R 1100 Boxer. The Boxer BMWs with their revolutionary chassis are successful, but they can still be seen as representing evolution. Honda hinted at a possible trend with the NR 750 oval-piston model. That one, of course, is not really meant for mass sale. But it shows that Honda can be expected to introduce some really novel bikes in the not-too-distant future. Suzuki has proved itself to be courageous in the past with the Wankel-inspired machine and the Katana. The fact that the first was a failure does not matter: Suzuki can deliver the goods. Kawasaki has so much economic power that the company seems unburstable. Whenever they want, they can invest in a revolutionary bike. Yamaha already has come up with a redefinition of the motorcycle in their GTS 1000. Its suspension, for example, is innovative; omission of the normal front fork in a production model is daring. And the absence, more or less, of a frame as well is pretty daring too. In fact the total approach is different. But perhaps Yamaha is too far ahead of its time. The public seems not to be ready for the GTS, for it is not a big seller. I can only regret this, for it is such a marvellous machine. I am absolutely sure that 25 years from now we will look with different eyes at a 'classic' GTS 1000. If the Japanese do not keep with this redefinition of the motorcycle, the Europeans will, or the Koreans. As the French say: History always repeats itself.

ACKNOWLEDGEMENTS

It should be clear that covering four decades of the history of the major part of the present-day motorcycle industry cannot be done without help! Further to my own experience, numerous books and brochures and people were consulted, either for information as such or as a second opinion. I don't feature in all the action photographs in this book; nonetheless, I rode all the bikes and the comments on machine behaviour and so on are entirely my own.

I wish to thank photographer Wout Meppelink, who knows virtually every GP rider in the world - and they all know him. Wout has vast experience in portraying motorcycles both on and off the race track. His work is on view in magazines and newspapers, worldwide.

I thank the representatives of the Big Four - Honda, Kawasaki, Yamaha and Suzuki - in various European countries, as well as in the USA. Ludy Beumer, of Yamaha Europe, kindly loaned the pictures of the 'never-on-the-market' RZ 201 and GL 750. Then there is the weekly magazine Motor (on sale since 1913); I was able to have access to their archives. I am indebted, dear colleagues! Another magazine, ProMotor, and photographer Chris Pennarts kindly cooperated when I came to writing about Bridgestones: I still enjoy working for and with both.

Colin MacKellar helped out in forming and shaping the text. Vivid discussions with him were very fruitful. Ralph Walker was an unfailing source of information on everything to do with Lilac/Marusho. Thanks to his "Newsletters" many puzzles were solved. Kiyoshi Nakagawa is the man who monitors the classic movement in the home country of our chosen motorcycles; he, too, was invaluable. Then there is Michael Buttinger, of Classic Motorcycle Supply, who came to me for advice on old Honda machines some years ago. Now he is a worldwide parts trader, and responsible for my collecting sales brochures and bikes so rare that I thought I should never even see, let alone own, them. He can be reached on 0031-35-6564492.

A quarter-century's studying and collecting adds up to a lot of information and fun en route. Having a houseful of documents and more than 50 bikes encompassing 15 makes (among which ten are Japanese) is deeply rewarding. Ten years experience as a motorcycle retailer helps as well - although I seem to carry on regularly learning something new. I should like to keep it that way; so comments, components or brochures are welcome! Fax me at my shop: (Holland) 0031-344-618345.

CORNELIS VANDENHEUVEL